Acknowledgments

Solution Tree Press would like to thank the following reviewers:

Tamara Chavez
English as a Second Language
  Teacher
Rio Rancho High School
Rio Rancho, New Mexico

Virginia Clayton
English as a Second Language
  Teacher
Northern High School
Durham, North Carolina

Susan Hall
President
95 Percent Group Inc.
Buffalo Grove, Illinois

Anne Katz
Consultant
Education Design Group
San Francisco, California

Janette Klingner
Professor, Department of Educational
  Equity and Cultural Diversity
University of Colorado
Boulder, Colorado

Shelley Archuleta Smith
English Language Development
  Curriculum Coordinator
Metropolitan Nashville Public Schools
Nashville, Tennessee

Implementing

RTI

with

ENGLISH LEARNERS

Douglas Fisher
Nancy Frey
Carol Rothenberg

Solution Tree | Press

a division of
Solution Tree

555 North Morton Street
Bloomington, IN 47404

800.733.6786 (toll free) / 812.336.7700
FAX: 812.336.7790

email: info@solution-tree.com
solution-tree.com

Printed in the United States of America

15 14 13 12 11   1 2 3 4 5

FSC
Mixed Sources
Product group from well-managed
forests and other controlled sources
Cert no. SW-COC-002283
www.fsc.org
© 1996 Forest Stewardship Council

Library of Congress Cataloging-in-Publication Data

Fisher, Douglas, 1965-
    Implementing RTI with English learners / Douglas Fisher, Nancy Frey, Carol Rothenberg.
        p. cm.
    Includes bibliographical references and index.
    ISBN 978-1-935249-97-9 (softbound) -- ISBN 978-1-935249-98-6 (library edition) 1. English language--Study and teaching--United States--Foreign speakers. 2. Language arts--Remedial teaching--United States. I. Frey, Nancy, 1959- II. Rothenberg, Carol. III. Title.
    PE1128.A2F54297 2011
    428.2'4--dc22
                                                        2010032343

Solution Tree
Jeffrey C. Jones, CEO & President

Solution Tree Press
President: Douglas M. Rife
Publisher: Robert D. Clouse
Vice President of Production: Gretchen Knapp
Managing Production Editor: Caroline Wise
Senior Production Editor: Risë Koben
Proofreader: David Eisnitz
Text Designer: Orlando Angel
Cover Designer: Pamela Rude

Table of Contents

About the Authors

DOUGLAS FISHER, PhD, is a professor of language and literacy education in the School of Teacher Education at San Diego State University and a teacher leader at Health Sciences High & Middle College. He is the recipient of an International Reading Association Celebrate Literacy Award, the Farmer Award for excellence in writing from the National Council of Teachers of English, and a Christa McAuliffe Award for excellence in teacher education from the American Association of State Colleges and Universities. He has published numerous articles on reading and literacy, differentiated instruction, and curriculum design, as well as books, including *Checking for Understanding: Formative Assessment Techniques for Your Classroom*; *Better Learning Through Structured Teaching: A Framework for the Gradual Release of Responsibility*; *Background Knowledge: The Missing Piece of the Comprehension Puzzle*; *In a Reading State of Mind: Brain Research, Teacher Modeling, and Comprehension Instruction*; and *Literacy 2.0: Reading and Writing in the 21st Century Classroom*.

NANCY FREY, PhD, is a professor of literacy in the School of Teacher Education at San Diego State University (SDSU) and a teacher leader at Health Sciences High & Middle College. She is the recipient of the 2008 Early Career Achievement Award from the National Reading Conference and a Christa McAuliffe Award for excellence in teacher education from the American Association of State Colleges and Universities. She has published in *The Reading Teacher, Journal of Adolescent and Adult Literacy, English Journal, Voices in the Middle, Middle School Journal, Remedial and Special Education,* and *Educational Leadership.* She is a coauthor of the books *Content-Area Conversations: How to Plan Discussion-Based Lessons for Diverse Language Learners, Learning Words Inside and Out,* and *Literacy*

2.0: Reading and Writing in the 21st Century Classroom. She teaches a variety of courses in SDSU's teacher-credentialing program on elementary and secondary reading instruction and literacy in content areas, classroom management, and supporting students with diverse learning needs.

CAROL ROTHENBERG is the coordinator of the New Arrival Center in the San Diego Unified School District, an intensive, accelerated program for adolescents who are new to English and new to the United States. She is also a consultant to the Springdale School District in Arkansas, where she has been a lead trainer for the districtwide initiative on literacy and English learners. She has worked with elementary and secondary schools throughout the San Diego Unified School District, training teachers and administrators on effective programs and instruction for EL students. An experienced classroom teacher and literacy coach with a master's degree in special education, Carol has taught bilingual special education, Spanish, ESL, and state-approved classes for teacher certification. She is the coauthor of *Language Learners in the English Classroom* and *Teaching English Language Learners: A Differentiated Approach.* As a member of the consultant network for NCTE, she helped develop the online professional development program *Pathways for Adolescent Literacy.*

Introduction

THIS BOOK IS ABOUT providing solutions for teaching English learners. We use response to intervention (RTI) as a framework to organize schoolwide improvement efforts, and we demonstrate how schools respond when students don't learn. Our focus is squarely on English learners and thus might veer slightly from accepted recommendations about RTI in general. Having said that, we do draw from the vast research base on RTI and effective instruction and intervention to situate our recommendations.

Helping students become proficient in English is a tall order. How many of us could move abroad, take a job in our chosen career, and be able to function well in that job if we needed to be able to communicate in an unfamiliar language? Teachers and administrators face a steep learning curve as our profession focuses on developing the knowledge, skills, and resources necessary for teaching culturally and linguistically diverse students.

The achievement data for English learners suggest that increased attention to this group of students is warranted. For example, the 2009 National Assessment of Educational Progress reading assessment indicated that 74 percent of eighth-grade English learners enrolled in public schools scored below the basic achievement level (National Center for Education Statistics, 2010). This compares with the 22 percent of non–English learners who scored below basic. Sadly, the 2009 scores for English learners show no growth when compared with the 1998 scores. State-level data also suggest a need for improvement. Even a cursory look at achievement trends in any state indicates that English learners lag behind their peers and are often the subgroup that fails to reach the expected levels of achievement (Abedi, 2004). Further, the performance assessment data suggest that significant numbers of English learners do not progress as expected in English language acquisition. It is clear that school systems are not yet providing instruction that meets the needs of a large number of English learners, despite many well-meaning attempts to do so.

When a student fails to make progress, adults tend to ask, "What's wrong with this kid?" The underlying factors in a student's lack of progress are often difficult to identify. In the absence of another idea, assumptions are made, and students who are not making progress are referred for special education testing. Determining the cause of an English learner's difficulties is particularly complicated. Many factors influence our ability to differentiate between "learning disability" and "language learning," including culture, the language acquisition process, and the availability of appropriate assessments in both the primary language (L1) and English.

The reauthorized Individuals with Disabilities Education Improvement Act (IDEA) of 2004 introduced RTI as a new option for identifying learning difficulties. The revised law changes the process of identification from focusing on the discrepancy between expected and current performance to focusing on instruction and the "child's response to scientific, research-based intervention" (US Department of Education, 2006, § 300.307[a][2]). The goal of RTI is to eliminate the possibility that a lack of access to quality instruction might explain persistent underachievement. Only when a struggling student fails to respond to progressively more intense levels of intervention is he or she referred for special education testing. Of particular importance for our focus here, the law clearly removes a student's lack of proficiency in English from the equation for defining the existence of a learning disability.

While special education services are a worthy topic, they are beyond the scope of this book. Supports for students who have disabilities and are culturally and linguistically diverse occupy a rich portion of special education research (see, for example, Harry & Klingner, 2005). Our attention is focused on RTI primarily as a means for articulating sound, culturally responsive teaching for English learners who are at risk for failure. Identification of students who qualify for specialized services is a by-product, and not the sole mission of, an approach to instruction and intervention. In the model discussed in this book, intervention is an element of good teaching and does not stand apart from what occurs daily in the classroom.

As we will explain in detail in subsequent chapters, the RTI model consists of three tiers of instruction and intervention. In brief, Tier 1, core instruction, is the regular class instruction that all students receive. Tier 2 provides struggling students with supplemental intervention that is designed to catch them up to grade-level expectations. Tier 3 intensifies the interventions for those who continue to experience difficulty.

Professional Learning Communities and RTI

The response to intervention model is also a tool for meaningful school improvement. As Khan and Mellard (2008) noted, "RTI can be viewed as a framework of system reform" (p. 4). When entire schools focus on RTI, intervention becomes systematized and coordinated. When teachers work together in professional learning communities (DuFour, DuFour, Eaker, & Karhanek, 2004) and focus on RTI, achievement increases and referrals to special education decrease.

In general, professional learning communities (PLCs) provide a structure for teachers and administrators to engage in a continuous improvement process to get results. PLCs give teachers an opportunity to focus on student work and to plan instruction based on student performance. PLCs are not simply extra meetings to attend but are an ongoing arrangement that allows teachers to engage with colleagues about students and their learning. Members of a PLC share a vision about their work, learn collaboratively with one another, visit and review other classrooms, and participate in decision making as it relates to teaching and learning.

There are a number of teams necessary to ensure that RTI is effective. In schools that operate as professional learning communities, subgroups meet as teams to accomplish specific tasks. It is very common to have grade-level teams or departments work together to align curriculum and instruction. In addition, in schools that have adopted RTI, there is often a team that focuses on the overall implementation of the model, coordinating professional development for teachers and system-level implementation of interventions. There is also often an assessment team that selects screening and progress-monitoring tools and reviews assessment results, especially for students whose learning problems are difficult to figure out. Some schools also have a student study team, a group of teachers who meet to make recommendations for instruction and intervention for students experiencing difficulty. Student study teams predate most RTI efforts and typically function in support of the overall PLC teams. Membership on these various teams depends on the school but always includes regular classroom teachers as well as specialists who provide additional information to the team.

From a PLC perspective, we can consider how the three tiers of RTI operate to inform policies, professional development, and continuous improvement. The system goal for Tier 1, core instruction, is that at least 70 percent of the students will reach expected performance levels. For English learners, this goal means that they gain, at minimum, a year of English proficiency for each year they are in school. It also means that they are making progress on state assessments. When 70 percent of the students do not reach the expected performance levels, the school or district PLC should focus on improving the quality of the core instruction. We focus on Tier 1, core instruction, in chapter 2.

School- or district-level PLC teams are crucial to the design of Tier 2 supplemental interventions for students in need. For English learners, Tier 2 interventions often focus on the English language, from phonemes and graphemes to vocabulary, pronunciation, and grammar. Members of PLC teams share effective practices with one another and can also examine student work collaboratively to make decisions about program effectiveness. We focus on Tier 2, supplemental intervention, in chapter 3.

Tier 3 intensive interventions can also be developed and delivered at the system level, as when every credentialed teacher is paired with an English learner and provides 1:1 instruction either before, during, or after school. Tier 3 efforts often focus on groups of students with similar needs who are not making progress. These efforts might address attendance and behavior as well as academics. For English learners, it is very common to provide Tier 3 interventions to students who have not been able to progress beyond intermediate levels of English proficiency. We focus on Tier 3, intensive intervention, in chapter 4.

This book provides a process for school improvement that PLCs can use, as well as specific guidelines for applying the RTI construct to the identification of English learners who need supplemental and intensive intervention, and perhaps a referral to determine eligibility for special education services. As with other RTI efforts, this system will ensure that students are not waiting to fail before they receive quality instruction and added interventions. Most importantly, though, an RTI approach is an instructional one, and the ultimate purpose is to ensure that the instruction is effective for the *individual child*. In each of the chapters that follow, we end with solutions that teachers, parents, and school systems can use to ensure that English learners access the core curriculum and achieve at high levels.

CHAPTER 1

Success With English Learners: It All Comes Down to Language

IT'S THE FIRST DAY OF SCHOOL. Kindergartners—hair neatly combed, brand-new school uniforms, shirts tucked in—arrive, holding their parents' hands. The parents leave their children with their new teacher in the lunch court with a few last words of encouragement and go off to their various responsibilities for the day. The few parents who linger to watch the start of the first day of school stand unobtrusively in the shadows so they won't distract their child or precipitate another round of tears.

Carol, a literacy coach at the school, helps the new kindergartners pick up their breakfast from the cafeteria. "Hola, Diana! ¿Qué quieres comer?" (What do you want to eat?) "¿Huevos o cereal con leche?" (Eggs or cereal with milk?) Reading from the nametags hung around the students' necks, she shows them the breakfast choices, queries each student, and directs them to the next cart to pick up their juice. With the students who don't speak English or Spanish, she asks them in English while she points to their choices.

Carol knows virtually nothing about any of the students, but she uses this cafeteria duty as an opportunity to watch and learn what she can about each of them. She watches Diana chatter away in Spanish with her friends and surmises that she is very verbal. She notices that Oscar reads the name off another student's nametag and learns that he knows something about reading.

Later, after all the students are in their respective classrooms, Carol sees one of the yard supervisors with a little boy in tow and joins them to see if she can help. In order to find out where Josué is supposed to be, she looks at her list of assignments and finds two Josués. When she asks the boy in a few different ways what his last name is, he responds, "No sé" (I don't know). Does this mean he doesn't understand her question? Or that he is so confused he doesn't understand what she wants? Or does he really not know his last name?

These are questions Carol obviously cannot answer after her first interaction with a student, but she stores away the information she does learn. Later, as she works with students in their classrooms, she can combine this information with her observations in various classroom contexts to compile a bigger picture. Future discussions with the students' teachers increase both

Carol's and the teachers' knowledge about the students and help to inform the classroom instruction.

This is where responsive teaching begins. It starts with knowing one's students and using that knowledge to design and adjust instruction to match their needs. Teachers must consider their students' background knowledge, learning styles and skills, and existing content knowledge. For English learners, they must also consider and address language proficiency levels, cultural differences, and prior experiences that might affect learning, particularly for students arriving from places where their education has been disrupted by war or poverty. This is what it means to ensure that students have the opportunity to learn. A major challenge is that English learners are not monolithic, and therefore the systems we design must be responsive to several types of students who are present even within the same school or classroom.

English Learners: Who Are They?

The five million immigrant students in US schools are a richly diverse group. They bring with them different languages, cultures, background experiences, academic skills, hopes, and dreams, and of course, they also bring different needs.

While it is important to consider each student individually, for the sake of discussion we can group EL students loosely into four categories:

1 Recent arrivals with high literacy in their primary language and little or no English

2 Recent arrivals with low literacy in their primary language and little or no English

3 Students who have lived in the United States a few years (two to five) and are on track to develop native-like proficiency in English

4 Long-term US residents who have little literacy in their primary language, adequate oral communication in English, and poor academic literacy skills in both languages

Recent arrivals with high literacy in their primary language and little or no English. Typically, these students already possess an understanding of how language works and know how to make meaning from text. They use a variety of strategies to facilitate learning. They are able to focus on their primary task of attaching a new lexicon and linguistic structure to familiar skills and ideas, and they rapidly develop English proficiency. They will probably be ready to participate successfully in grade-level mainstream classes within a short time, varying of course by individual. Importantly, despite their skills, they will still need focused language instruction along with support in their core content-area classes. In general, we will not see these students referred for special education evaluation.

Recent arrivals with low literacy in their primary language and little or no English. This group of students, while certainly not the majority of English learners, poses a significantly greater challenge to teachers. Because they lack foundational academic knowledge and skills, they often must learn basic concepts of reading and writing at the same time as they are learning a new language and a new way of life. Many districts have created newcomer centers to address the unique needs of these students. These centers are meant to provide an intensive short-term program that equips beginning English learners with tools for continued content learning. Instruction is designed to move students to a threshold level of English proficiency that will enable them to engage successfully in grade-level instruction. However, we caution that without careful long-range planning that includes clear entry and exit criteria and procedures, there is a risk that this approach could create a marginalized and segregated educational setting (Feinberg, 2000).

Students who have lived in the United States two to five years and are approaching native-like proficiency in English. These students may not yet be proficient in English or performing at grade level in their core content classes, but they are progressing as expected along the continuum of language development and are able to access the important concepts and ideas. They will need focused language instruction aimed at their proficiency level, as well as continued support to access the key content and ideas in the core subjects. Some may be moving more slowly through the levels of language proficiency than others; however, as long as they continue to progress, they generally should not be considered for special education.

Long-term US residents who have little literacy in their primary language, adequate oral communication in English, and poor academic literacy skills in both languages. This group is the largest group of English learners in US schools, particularly secondary schools. It includes students who may have been in the US school system since kindergarten but, for a variety of reasons, have not attained grade-level literacy. They have typically reached a level of language proficiency that allows them to communicate adequately in informal situations with their peers but not in academic contexts. These students become increasingly noticeable as they move up through the grades, are offered fewer supports for learning, and begin to flounder amid the more rigorous academic demands (Chall, Jacobs, & Baldwin, 1990).

The broad range of English learners in US schools seems to require an appropriately nuanced definition of proficiency, but that idea has not been universally accepted. Educators and linguists have approached the issue of proficiency from several directions, and their attention to various aspects of language and learning has alternately resulted in conflict and convergence.

What Does It Mean to Be Proficient in a Language?

Over the years, educators have defined and redefined the term *proficient* in multiple ways. Cummins (1979) proposed a useful construct that divided language into two dimensions: social and academic. He highlighted the differences in the length of time required to develop the two types of language, as well as the differences in how they are acquired and the dominant skills each relies upon. This construct helped educators understand why we might think a student is proficient in English when we have a casual conversation with her and then wonder why she doesn't seem to really understand the class work. Cummins labeled these two dimensions of language BICS (Basic Interpersonal Communication Skills) and CALP (Cognitive Academic Language Proficiency). As a field, we began to recognize that academic language seemed to require many different competencies from social language and that the two dimensions of language encompassed a vastly different range of cognitive demands and contextual support.

Our understanding of language proficiency has continued to evolve since then. We recognize that social and academic language are acquired concurrently. We now know that, while the two kinds of language are different in many ways, many of the language skills required in social contexts are also useful in academic contexts. And we would argue that language can be acquired more quickly than research suggests. While our understanding of the definition of language proficiency has grown significantly, it is still commonly accepted that it takes one to two years to acquire social language and five to seven years to acquire academic language; some experts believe that the latter may take as long as ten years for some students (see, for example, Thomas & Collier, 2002). The limited research available on the topic corroborates these timelines. But it is our belief that, if the findings were based on studies of existing programs and practice, then what the research tells us is what *has been*, not what *can be*. As we talk to educators across the country, it is difficult to find evidence of comprehensive programs that are considered to be models of best practice across the school day and over the years a child is in school. Certainly there are outstanding teachers and successful programs, but when one examines a child's schooling over the course of several years, it is not often that he or she has participated in outstanding long-term language development programs. We would suggest that it is entirely possible that, given the opportunity to participate consistently in an outstanding program that implements research-based best practice, a student would progress along a much-accelerated timeline of language development.

While a precise timeline may still be up for debate, most experts in the field, including Cummins, talk about a much more complex picture of proficiency than the two dimensions of social and academic language proposed in 1979. Canale and Swain (1980) offered a model of language proficiency consisting of four aspects: grammatical, sociolinguistic, discourse, and strategic. Canale (1983) labeled this construct "communicative competence," that is, the ability to communicate successfully in any context, be it social, academic, oral, or written. Canale and Swain's model included aspects of proficiency such as using language flexibly and in appropriate ways to achieve desired results within diverse contexts.

In 2000, Kern proposed an even more encompassing conceptual framework of literacy and language proficiency, one that defines "a broader discourse competence that involves the ability to interpret and critically evaluate a wide variety of written and spoken texts" (p. 2). He focused on proficiency in academic language and described not only its linguistic dimension but also its cognitive and cultural dimensions. Scarcella (2003) extended Kern's definition by identifying the specific components of each of these three dimensions of language proficiency. Scarcella described the skills, knowledge, critical thinking, and metacognitive awareness that students must develop to become proficient in academic English. Within this framework, she also included an understanding of the cultural values and beliefs that influence language, as well as the ability to use language strategically.

So what does all this theory translate into when we evaluate an EL student's use of language? Traditionally, we continue to judge proficiency in language by the student's use of grammar and vocabulary. Most rubrics are holistic and are used to score student writing in broad strokes, such as ideas, organization, voice, word choice, sentence fluency, and conventions (grammar and punctuation). And because that's what we assess, that's what we teach. As students move up through the grades, we tend to teach less grammar, assuming that they have already learned it.

If, however, we move beyond a simple linguistic definition of language and recognize it as the integration of a myriad of complex processes, then to evaluate proficiency, we must also look at students' knowledge base, critical thinking, and metacognitive skills. Of course this view of proficiency applies to the instruction of all students, not just English learners, but there are additional implications for helping non-native speakers of English develop their skills across all aspects of language. In each aspect of language, EL students may encounter challenges that native speakers do not face. The strategic use of language, for instance, requires an expansive lexis along with knowledge of how to use vocabulary and language structure *flexibly* in order to achieve a desired result. English learners may not have a wide range of vocabulary, adequate facility with language structure, or sufficient understanding of the nuances of words and the ways in which they can be arranged.

Acquisition Versus Learning: Approaches to Language Development

Just as our definition of language proficiency has evolved over the years, so has our definition of best practice in language instruction. Today, we have specific approaches for teaching school-age immigrant children who must learn a new language for academic success. It is important to note that historically, approaches to teaching English as a second language were informed by the practices for teaching native English speakers a "foreign" language (one that is spoken outside their own country). Though these approaches formed the genesis of modern-day ESL (English as a second language) or ESOL (English for speakers of other languages) instruction, prior to the 1970s they were not widely implemented with non-native schoolchildren, who were commonly left to their own devices when it came to learning English. Since then, approaches to second-language (L2) development have bifurcated based on the language of instruction in the classroom.

Instruction in English: ESL/ESOL/ELD

A predominant program model for English learners in US schools features English as the language of instruction. Students new to the language are taught using strategies such as Total Physical Response (Asher, 1966) and the use of real objects (realia), while those who have progressed further along the continuum of language development are taught using a cluster of instructional strategies collectively referred to as Specially Designed Academic Instruction in English (SDAIE). These techniques include practices such as building background and vocabulary knowledge, contextualizing new information, modeling, and offering experiences in multiple modalities. These instructional routines are intended to offer a language "shelter" to students who are learning both the content and the language simultaneously; in some places they are formally called Sheltered English classes. In addition, specific attention is given to English language development (ELD) to acquire the oral and written structures needed in social and academic contexts. Other terms, used at the secondary level, include English as a second language, and English for speakers of other languages.

Whether we call it ELD, ESL, ESOL, or Sheltered English, language instruction—from the earliest levels of proficiency—should integrate all four domains of language: listening, speaking, reading, and writing. When students first begin to learn English, instruction should focus on the skills they need for survival in both social and academic situations. Generally speaking, students move beyond this beginning level fairly rapidly. As they progress in their proficiency, instruction should turn to developing the higher level of language needed for success in the content areas. This is the foundational language that will help students understand and participate in grade-level learning. Their English instruction should be closely aligned with the grade-level English language arts program, facilitating their development of grade-level skills in literacy. As students reach more advanced levels of proficiency, there are often gaps in their ability to comprehend and produce academic English at the levels required in school. At this point, their ELD instruction must identify these gaps and provide opportunities for students to practice the language skills that will fill the gaps.

Clearly, we know far more about teaching language than we did even at the start of the twenty-first century. Since the advent of No Child Left Behind in 2001, the progress of English learners has received far more attention. In a report to the Carnegie Corporation, Short and Fitzsimmons (2007) identified challenges these students face but also named several teaching practices that were consistently successful in the literacy development of EL students. Among others, they recommended that teachers responsible for the literacy instruction of English learners:

- Integrate listening, speaking, reading, and writing skills
- Teach components and processes of reading and writing
- Teach reading comprehension strategies
- Focus on vocabulary development
- Build and activate background knowledge
- Teach language through content and themes
- Use the native language strategically (Short & Fitzsimmons, 2007, p. 38)

A fundamental aspect of language learning is proficiency in oral language. Overlooked in the classroom all too often, in deference to efficiency, oral language is essential to the development of proficiency in written language. In fact, we would offer that oracy is the foundation of literacy. An in-depth review of the research conducted by the National Literacy Panel on Language-Minority Children and Youth found that while EL students benefit from instruction in the key components of reading, that is not sufficient to develop proficiency (August & Shanahan, 2006). The panel noted the key role that oral proficiency plays in developing literacy skills. It found that oral proficiency in English is vital to developing proficiency in reading and writing English and, furthermore, that oral proficiency in the primary language accelerates this process.

Instruction in the Native Language: Bilingual Programs

Bilingual programs are based on the idea that literacy in the native language facilitates development of literacy in another language. There are also clear cultural and socioemotional benefits to developing and maintaining students' primary language literacy, benefits that in turn contribute to developing literacy in English. One of these benefits is that when teachers can communicate and teach in the students' primary language, they can easily build on the students' prior knowledge and skills, especially those that transfer across languages, such as phonemic awareness, reading strategies, and some vocabulary. Older students in particular, who already know quite a bit about how language works, can quickly transfer this knowledge from their primary language to English.

The amount and purpose of instruction in English varies according to the type of program, though all programs provide explicit instruction in English for the purpose of learning English. In bilingual programs, teachers may use English as the language of instruction in different ways, such as for review, vocabulary development, teaching core content following a preview and preceding a review in the primary language, or simply alternating subjects or units of study between English and the primary language. Most bilingual programs increase the amount of instruction in English each year as students gain more proficiency in English and more literacy and content knowledge in their primary language. This approach is often called a Late-Exit or Developmental Bilingual Program—that is, one that strategically transitions students from learning in their primary language to learning in English. Another program design that has been shown to be effective is Two-Way (or Dual) Immersion, in which a relatively equal number of minority-language and majority-language speakers are in class together and learn in both languages. While there is still a paucity of research in this area, one significant long-term study found that these two types of programs were the most effective in bringing students to high levels of achievement in both English and the minority language (Collier & Thomas, 2004).

In its review of the research, the National Literacy Panel found evidence that EL students receiving instruction in their native language perform better, on average, on English reading assessments than those receiving English-only instruction (August & Shanahan, 2006). Of course, it is not always feasible to provide a bilingual program; there simply is not a sufficient supply of certificated bilingual teachers in the multitude of languages that our students speak. So a large majority of EL students in the United States must continue to receive their instruction only in English. We believe in the socioemotional and academic power of bilingual education, and we encourage schools to establish bilingual programs when possible. However, we also know that all English learners, even those in bilingual programs, need instruction *in* English and *of* English.

Opportunities to Learn Language

If students are to attain a high level of proficiency that enables them to understand and express complex ideas in sophisticated ways, they need a focused approach that addresses the linguistic, cognitive, and sociocultural dimensions of language through both explicit instruction and authentic practice. Students must *use* language in order to *learn* language. We can accelerate their language learning by teaching them to reflect on their use of language, helping them develop metalinguistic skills that they can apply in support of meaning-making and critical thinking (for example, analyzing, predicting, solving problems). Students must learn how English works and then have many opportunities to use language if they are to reach the level of proficiency they need to succeed in grade-level work.

Function, Form, and Fluency: What Do Students Need to Know and Be Able to Do?

In classrooms one will find an array of methodologies based both on teachers' knowledge of language instruction and their beliefs about how language is acquired. One teacher might have a master's degree in ESL/ESOL, another might be a high school English teacher whose education courses focused on literature, and another might be an elementary school teacher who knows a great deal about teaching reading but little about teaching language. Teaching language is not the same as teaching in a high school English class or teaching first-grade students how to read. Effective instructional approaches for English learners, regardless of the district's programs and approaches, should address specific content through specific strategies that support and promote language development.

Dutro and Moran (2003) developed a model for instruction that proposes three specific areas of focused instruction: function, form, and fluency. This model offers a clear and concrete framework for instruction in the linguistic, cognitive, and sociocultural dimensions of language. We will briefly define function, form, and fluency.

Function

We use language for specific purposes, whether to introduce ourselves, ask a question, describe where we went on vacation, explain a math problem, recount an event in history, analyze a piece of literature, or hypothesize about possible outcomes of an experiment. Each of these purposes requires not only specific vocabulary but also certain language structures that serve each particular purpose. In other words, for each function of language, we must know the appropriate vocabulary and grammar to make our communication clear or to accurately interpret the communication of others.

Planning for effective language instruction requires identifying the purpose of the communication first and then organizing the learning tasks around that purpose, recognizing of course that we often use a variety of language functions as we communicate. In writing a persuasive essay, for instance, we must propose and describe solutions. We might further provide counterclaims, summarize, and so on. Once we are clear about the purpose, we can determine the language structures, or forms, that are typically used for that purpose.

Form

As in any undertaking, form follows function. We determine our purpose and then decide how we can best accomplish it. When playing tennis, if we want to hit a backhand shot (function), we shift our grip (form). In a baseball game, the pitcher will throw a curve or a fastball (form) depending on the kind of batter at the plate and whether he aims to strike him out or let him walk (function). And in language, we use specific language structures and vocabulary (form) to accomplish a particular purpose (function), changing our language depending on the purpose of the communication.

Form consists of both vocabulary and language structure. In teaching vocabulary, as we identify the topic vocabulary we must also identify the functional vocabulary that links the ideas and achieves the intended purpose. We often refer to this distinction in vocabulary as "bricks" (topic) and "mortar" (functional) (Dutro & Moran, 2003). The words we commonly teach—words like *mitosis, angle, democracy,* or *foreshadowing*—are the bricks. Mortar is also necessary to express the content—words like *if, therefore,* or *in spite of.* In other words, the mortar is the language that defines the relationship between ideas, events, actions, people, and things—the bricks.

Using proper language structures requires both knowledge of correct syntax and facility with the mortar vocabulary that promotes the intended purpose, or function, of the communication. Different functions of language, particularly academic uses of language, typically require specific forms of language. To sequence information, for example, we use words like *before, when, first* (mortar). To compare or contrast two items, we may use the comparative or superlative form of a word—*larger, largest* (mortar). When we describe, we might need to consider the shades of meaning of words—did the man *stride* (brick) across the room? Or did he *stroll* (brick) across the room? Language structure can also change according to the function. The function of making a prediction might use one form of a verb, as in "I think it *will be* [mortar] an interesting movie." Conversely, the function of expressing an opinion might use another form of the same verb, as in "I think it *would have been* [mortar] an interesting movie if it *hadn't been* [mortar] so long."

Fluency

We may know which forms to use with which functions, but we also need to be able to understand and use language with ease and accuracy. We call this skill fluency. It is the ability to string the words together quickly and adeptly in ways that do not sound awkward to the native speaker. When we hear the term *fluency* we tend to think of reading fluency—reading rapidly enough to maintain comprehension. Equally important to proficiency in academic language are oral and written fluency. Being able to find the right word to express ideas rather than having to rely on circuitous explanations to arrive at the desired point is part of both written and oral fluency. Students need to be able to speak and write in ways that clearly, succinctly, and effectively express ideas, thoughts, and information. Reaching fluency requires multiple and diverse opportunities to use language in authentic contexts.

Language Proficiency Levels

When students are able to use the functions and forms of language fluently, we consider them to be proficient. Reaching proficiency generally requires moving through a continuum, or series of levels, of increasing skill and understanding. While students may progress at different rates in different aspects of language as they develop proficiency, we can group them into a general progression of levels for instructional and assessment purposes.

Many states have developed their own sets of standards for these proficiency levels, calling them by a variety of names, such as beginning, early intermediate, intermediate, early advanced, and advanced (in California) or levels 1, 2, 3, 4, and 5 (in several other states). TESOL (Teachers of English to Speakers of Other Languages) has provided a widely accepted description of five levels: starting, emerging, developing, expanding, and bridging (see table 1.1, page 16).

Goals for English Language Development and Instruction

Clearly, the goal for all of our students is to meet grade-level content standards. When students are learning English at the same time as they are learning content, however, we need benchmarks that define their pathway toward the standards. WIDA (World-Class Instructional Design and Assessment), a consortium of twenty states, developed a set of preK–12 English Language Proficiency standards addressing the dual goals for English learners: proficiency in English and achievement in the core content areas. These standards set expectations for communication and language use in five areas: mathematics, language arts, science, social studies, and social and instructional purposes (WIDA, 2004/2007). The WIDA standards provided the foundation for the standards developed by TESOL, which built upon and augmented the key ideas (TESOL, 2006). The TESOL standards define the central role of language in content-area achievement, highlighting the particular instructional and assessment needs of learners who are still developing proficiency in English (see table 1.2, page 17). As such, they serve to complement discipline-specific standards in the core content areas, describing the language to expect and offering examples of appropriate tasks in each subject at the various levels

Table 1.1: TESOL's Five Levels of Proficiency

Starting	Students initially have limited or no understanding of English. They rarely use English for communication. They respond nonverbally to simple commands, statements, and questions. As their oral comprehension increases, they begin to imitate the verbalizations of others by using single words or simple phrases, and they begin to use English spontaneously. At the earliest stage, these learners construct meaning from text primarily through illustrations, graphs, maps, and tables.
Emerging	Students can understand phrases and short sentences. They can communicate limited information in simple everyday and routine situations by using memorized phrases, groups of words, and formulae. They can use selected simple structures correctly but still systematically produce basic errors. Students begin to use general academic vocabulary and familiar everyday expressions. Errors in writing are present that often hinder communication.
Developing	Students understand more complex speech but still may require some repetition. They use English spontaneously but may have difficulty expressing all their thoughts due to a restricted vocabulary and a limited command of language structure. Students at this level speak in simple sentences, which are comprehensible and appropriate, but which are frequently marked by grammatical errors. Proficiency in reading may vary considerably. Students are most successful constructing meaning from texts for which they have background knowledge upon which to build.
Expanding	Students' language skills are adequate for most day-to-day communication needs. They communicate in English in new or unfamiliar settings but have occasional difficulty with complex structures and abstract academic concepts. Students at this level may read with considerable fluency and are able to locate and identify the specific facts within the text. However, they may not understand texts in which the concepts are presented in a decontextualized manner, the sentence structure is complex, or the vocabulary is abstract or has multiple meanings. They can read independently but may have occasional comprehension problems, especially when processing grade-level information.
Bridging	Students can express themselves fluently and spontaneously on a wide range of personal, general, academic, or social topics in a variety of contexts. They are poised to function in an environment with native speaking peers with minimal language support or guidance. Students have a good command of technical and academic vocabulary as well as idiomatic expressions and colloquialisms. They can produce clear, smoothly flowing, well-structured texts of differing lengths and degrees of linguistic complexity. Errors are minimal, difficult to spot, and generally corrected when they occur.

Source: TESOL (2006). Used with permission.

of proficiency. The sample performance indicators can serve as a useful tool to guide content instruction and language support for students at any level of proficiency in English. More information about the standards can be found at www.tesol.org.

Table 1.2: TESOL's PreK–12 English Language Proficiency Standards

Standard 1	English language learners **communicate** for **social, intercultural, and instructional** purposes within the school setting.
Standard 2	English language learners **communicate** information, ideas, and concepts necessary for academic success in the area of **language arts**.
Standard 3	English language learners **communicate** information, ideas, and concepts necessary for academic success in the area of **mathematics**.
Standard 4	English language learners **communicate** information, ideas, and concepts necessary for academic success in the area of **science**.
Standard 5	English language learners **communicate** information, ideas, and concepts necessary for academic success in the area of **social studies**.

Source: TESOL (2006). Used with permission.

What About Students Who Don't Seem to Be Making Progress?

Although we know that the development of a subsequent language takes several years of purposeful instruction, some students seem to fall behind others. They cause concern to their teachers and families, who worry about their future success. To complicate things further, students who are learning English often offer a profile that is similar to a student who has a language or learning disability (Brice & Brice, 2009; Case & Taylor, 2005). A response to intervention approach makes sense for students who may need further instruction to *prevent* school failure, as opposed to using RTI solely to *identify* students for special education (Johnston, 2010).

Common implementation models of RTI involve three tiers of instruction and intervention (Ardoin, Witt, Connell, & Koenig, 2005; Buffum, Mattos, & Weber, 2009). As graphically displayed in figure 1.1 (page 18), the three-tier model assumes that fewer and fewer students will need supplemental and intensive intervention. It also suggests that interventions require intensifying time, expertise, assessment, and family involvement. We'll return to this graphic to organize the contents of the subsequent chapters.

Tier 1, core instruction, is the regular classroom instruction that all students receive. (This does not mean that all students receive the same instruction,

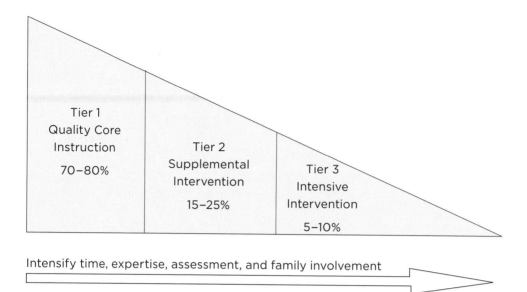

Figure 1.1: Tiers of instruction and intervention.

because core instruction accommodates differentiation. But differentiation within Tier 1 is not considered to be intervention.) Core instruction should be evidence-based, relevant to student needs, and consistent with grade-level standards. As part of Tier 1, teachers use screening measures to identify students who are experiencing difficulty. In addition, teachers use progress-monitoring tools to identify students who are falling behind and who may need supplemental intervention.

Tier 2 provides students with supplemental intervention that is designed to catch them up to grade-level expectations. These interventions can be provided as part of the regular class day, as in added small-group instruction, or scheduled beyond the school day as part of before- or after-school activities. The regular classroom teacher can provide these supplemental interventions, as can special educators, Title I teachers, reading specialists, or English learner support teachers. The frequency of progress-monitoring assessments increases and is at least monthly but can be more often. In a typical classroom, 15 to 25 percent of the students will need supplemental intervention at some point in the year. The key to Tier 2 intervention is to ensure that the student also participates in the core instruction provided as part of Tier 1. Otherwise, the student is likely to fall further behind his or her classmates and to require long-term interventions.

Tier 3 interventions are much more intensive, are often individualized, and require weekly or more frequent assessments. These interventions can be provided during the school day, when experts can push services into the classroom, such as when the Title I teacher or reading specialist provides individualized instruction as part of the overall reading lesson all students receive. When Tier 3 interventions fail to address a student's learning needs, a referral for special education services is considered. In a typical school, 5 to 10 percent of the students will need intensive intervention at some point in the year. When either PLC or student study team members meet to consider a special education referral, they can draw on the data that were collected during Tier 2 and 3 interventions.

In some places, RTI is described as a four-tier model, with the fourth tier representing special education supports and services (Klingner & Edwards, 2006). We believe this is a useful construct for illustrating the nature of RTI as a measurement and identification system, but not as useful when it comes to its function as an instructional system. Johnston (2010) states:

> Framed as a strategy for *identifying* students with LD, RTI becomes a *measurement* problem. . . . Framed as a strategy for *preventing* LD, RTI becomes an *instructional* problem, emphasizing responsive teaching and the most instructionally useful assessment, and providing the means and context for improving teaching and teacher expertise. (p. 602)

Four English Learners

We would like to introduce four students, English learners who can help us move from a theoretical discussion to a more personalized view of the implementation of RTI. We will follow each of their stories in subsequent chapters. After all, it is all about the students.

Seyo: First-grade student from Eritrea, arrived at age three, early intermediate proficiency

Seyo arrived in the United States with her family while she was still a toddler. Her home language is Tigrinya, and her family engages in lots of storytelling about the family, as well as passing down tales in the oral tradition. Her family arrived in an area with an active community support system, and within a short time Seyo was enrolled in the local Head Start program. Her family values education, and although her parents do not have a strong command of English themselves, they have been able to participate in schooling decisions with the aid of the school district and fellow community members. After a year of preschool, Seyo attended a full-day kindergarten program at her neighborhood school. She is shy by nature and seems reluctant to participate in class discussions, although she is outgoing and friendly on the playground. Now in first grade, she has made little progress in reading acquisition.

Yazmin: *Third-grade student from Michoacán, Mexico, arrived in first grade, early intermediate proficiency*

Yazmin arrived in first grade with no English. Now she speaks in single words and short, simple sentences. Her writing is disorganized and difficult to comprehend because of many errors in word choice, verb tense, and syntax. In first and second grades she received twenty minutes a day of ELD instruction and was often absent due to chronic health problems.

Eduardo: *Seventh-grade student from a border town, arrived at the beginning of fourth grade, intermediate proficiency*

Eduardo was born in the United States, just inside the border with Mexico. After a few months his family crossed the border back into Mexico and lived with Eduardo's uncle and his family. When he was six years old, Eduardo began school; he attended school in Mexico through the third grade, when his father had an opportunity for a job in the United States. The family moved back across the border, and Eduardo enrolled in fourth grade that fall. He was placed in a classroom with many other Spanish-speaking students and a few students from Vietnam, the Philippines, and Somalia. Most of his classmates had been in the school since kindergarten or first grade and were at the developing level of English proficiency. During the English language arts (ELA) block, a teacher pulled Eduardo and two other students out of class and spent thirty minutes teaching them beginning-level English vocabulary and grammar. Eduardo has worked hard in class and communicates orally, with the typical mistakes a student at the developing level would make. He can express most of his ideas in writing but uses very simple vocabulary and sentence construction. Though he enjoys graphic novels, he does not complete homework assignments that require reading.

Minh: *Ninth-grade student from Vietnam, arrived in second grade, early intermediate proficiency*

When Minh arrived in the United States, she was seven years old and spoke no English. She enrolled in school in September and was placed in a second-grade class with twenty-seven other starting- and emerging-level English learners. The class received English language development (ELD) instruction for twenty minutes each day. The remainder of the day followed a typical second-grade curriculum with three hours of ELA, one hour of math, and the remaining hours alternating between social studies, science, health, PE, and art. The majority of the class was Spanish-speaking, though there were two other students from Vietnam, a boy named Duy and a girl named Trina. Duy and Trina had attended the school in first grade and could speak some English. The teacher seated Minh next to Trina and Duy to help her understand the class discussions and assignments. Minh was very shy in class and participated very little, although on the playground with Trina, she ran, played, and chatted.

Now a ninth-grader, Minh works very hard and spends hours every night on her homework. Her oral English is very difficult to understand, and her eighth-grade teacher reports that she saw no improvement in Minh's writing during the previous year. After seven years of schooling in the United States, Minh scores at level 3 (intermediate) on the state ELD assessment, but just barely above the cut point for that level.

Where to Start

So what does it take to become proficient in English? We begin with recognizing that learning language requires far more than sitting with a tutor for twenty minutes three or four days a week and identifying pictures of food, body parts, or modes of transportation. And it surely takes more than merely being exposed to English throughout the day. As a start, we suggest two solutions for teaching English learners.

SOLUTIONS FOR TEACHING ENGLISH LEARNERS

1. All teachers view themselves as language teachers. Lest readers think that we are suggesting that math teachers need to be language teachers, let us elaborate. If part of our definition of academic language is being able to understand and use the language of each content area, then all teachers must be cognizant of the language that is used in the content areas they teach. How do mathematicians talk and write? Scientists? Historians? There are different norms for the organization of language in different content areas. This means that not only does the vocabulary of the content areas differ, but also the language functions and thus the forms. Mathematicians are typically concise, commonly using functions such as sequencing or cause and effect. Textbooks often use the passive voice, a manner of expression that we don't tend to use in everyday conversations and that is somewhat more difficult to understand than the active voice. For example:

Passive: The problem was solved by the students.

Active: The students solved the problem.

Everyday words may have different meanings in math than in conversation, and some words may even signal a different mathematical operation, depending on how the problem is stated. Look at the following two examples:

1. Raul has five dollars. Ana has three. How much less money does Ana have than Raul?

2. Ana has three dollars. She has two dollars less than Raul. How much money does Raul have?

Notice that in problem 1, *less* signals subtraction, whereas in problem 2, the same word signals addition.

Teachers in content areas must always be aware of the language the students need to know in order to understand the content and express that understanding. Similarly, language teachers must be aware of that same language used in the content area so that they can provide explicit instruction and practice using familiar content to develop language that can then be transferred to the new content.

2. All teachers know the proficiency levels of their students. There is a common understanding among educators that we need to know our students in order to be able to effectively design instruction that meets their needs. For English learners, that includes knowing their proficiency levels. It also means understanding what that proficiency level means in order to understand how to best support students at different levels of proficiency, to know what kinds of responses one should expect, and to identify prerequisite knowledge needed for successful participation in the lesson. This kind of differentiated support may include some preteaching or reteaching, purposeful pairing with students who can help with comprehension, partially completed graphic organizers, word banks, and books or websites on the same content but easier to understand, to name just a few.

When students are at early levels of language proficiency, they can learn grade-level content with specially designed instruction, but they still may miss some of the content as they strive to learn both content and language simultaneously. Providing opportunity to learn includes helping students fill in these gaps. Opportunity to learn for English learners means that we are aware of and provide for their needs in learning content and that we teach language explicitly.

CHAPTER 2

Tier 1: An Opportunity to Learn

"IF STUDENTS HAVE EQUAL opportunities to learn, doesn't that mean they have equal access?"

"Isn't effective instruction for English learners really just good teaching that works for all students?"

"Aren't instructional strategies for English learners the same ones we use for students with disabilities?"

"I never received ESOL, and I learned English. Shouldn't students now be able to do the same thing?"

Ask a group of educators to answer these questions, and you will surely hear affirmative and negative responses to each. It seems that everyone has an opinion about teaching students whose native language is not English, as well as about where to draw the line between the school's responsibility and that of the student and family. The mere mention of teaching English learners can evoke strong emotional responses, especially in an era of high-stakes testing and accountability for all students. These questions are at the very heart of the definition of *opportunity to learn*. If we were to answer yes to all of them, then the next logical step would be to bypass Tier 1 altogether for English learners and jump immediately to Tier 2 supplemental intervention, or even to Tier 3 intensive intervention. If schools with large English learner populations followed this approach, the RTI wedge that we presented in chapter 1 (page 18) would be reversed and might look something like the one in Figure 2.1 (page 24). But this would result in an inefficient, costly, and discriminatory way of educating children who are learning English.

Some would argue that, at the very least, *any* support for EL students falls within the bounds of Tier 2. After all, the federal laws that mandate instruction of English and core content say that a school must "take appropriate steps to overcome language barriers that impede equal participation by its students in its instructional programs" (Equal Educational Opportunities Act, 1974). There are, of course, many ways to define what constitutes "appropriate steps."

However, the learning of both language and content begins in the core program, and the classroom instructional design and curriculum should be crafted to reflect this principle. We interpret this to mean that it is the core program, or Tier 1, that provides the differentiated curriculum and instruction

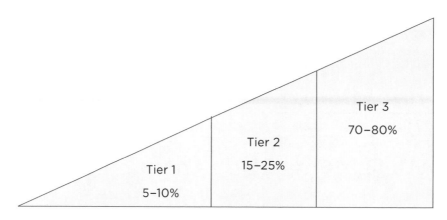

Figure 2.1: A reversal of the RTI process.

that give English learners equal access. Thus it is the core program that provides both English language development and access to grade-level content. And accordingly, before we look for interventions, we must be sure that Tier 1 instruction includes sufficient opportunity to learn both language and grade-level core content.

We believe that there are certain elements that must be present when teaching English learners, be it in English, in the students' primary language, or a combination of both. In this chapter, we describe a framework for instruction within which one can fit virtually any model or method of instruction one chooses. That is to say, within this framework, teachers can, and should, design their lessons strategically and responsively.

Effective Instruction for English Learners

A foundational assumption of education for English learners is that they have access to sound, evidence-based instruction that is aligned with grade-level standards. As we have noted, in a response to intervention model, this is referred to as Tier 1. The California Department of Education (2009) defines Tier 1 as instruction focused on grade-level benchmarks, or instruction within the core program. Other states throughout the country define Tier 1 similarly, and this has direct implications for students learning English. An RTI framework published by the National Center for Culturally Responsive Educational Systems notes that RTI for EL students is based on the premise that "effective and research-based instruction already occurs in the general education classroom for *all* students" and stresses that "effective and appropriate assessment as well as instruction must be both *linguistically* and *culturally* congruent" (Brown & Doolittle, 2008, p. 6).

In order to meet the needs of the wide diversity of learners in our classrooms, Tier 1 includes differentiated small-group instruction to help *all* students meet grade-level standards. For English learners, this means that Tier 1 must include one of a variety of research-based approaches to English language development and instruction. Whether schools provide instruction only in English, English with support in the primary language, Sheltered English Immersion, Late-Exit or Two-Way Bilingual, Content-Based ESL, or any of a number of other research-based approaches, the objective remains the same—to provide English learners with English language development and access to grade-level core curriculum.

Which of these programs works best for students has long been a hot topic for debate among educators, parents, community members, and legislators alike and is beyond the scope of this book. What is clear, however, is that each of these approaches can be implemented within Tier 1, or core instruction. While one of the components of RTI is fidelity to evidence-based instructional practices, federal law does not recommend specific models. Thus schools are able to tailor instruction to meet students' needs through the purposeful implementation of research-based practices. We have developed an instructional framework that draws on several decades' worth of research and offer it as a necessary component of Tier 1 instruction. Without quality core instruction, student needs will overwhelm the intervention system, and schools will not be able to demonstrate the achievement gains expected of them.

A Framework for Instruction: The Gradual Release of Responsibility Model

Regardless of the approach, model, or language used in the classroom, effective instruction for EL students relies on several common practices. The Center for Research on Education, Diversity and Excellence identified five standards for effective pedagogy that we find in some way, shape, or form in virtually every description of quality instruction that we see. These five standards emerged from principles of practice found to be successful over decades of implementation with both majority and minority at-risk students (Dalton, 1998; Tharp, 1997). Various instructional models may label and organize their key ideas differently, but we find these standards of teaching practice embedded within all of them:

1 Teachers and students producing together

2 Developing language and literacy across the curriculum

3 Making lessons meaningful

4 Teaching complex thinking

5 Teaching through conversation

The framework we use in classrooms and across schools to articulate these standards is also a means for providing a structure for instruction. It is based on the *gradual release of responsibility* model in reading comprehension described by Pearson and Gallagher (1983). Our gradual release of responsibility framework is built on the premise that the goal of instruction is competent student independence. Graves and Fitzgerald (2003) suggest that "it is through this process of gradually assuming more and more responsibility for their learning that students become competent, independent learners" (p. 98). In order to do so, students must be able to access the appropriate knowledge or select the appropriate skill to match each situation that arises. As the name of the framework implies, students gain this independence through a gradual shift in cognitive responsibility.

This method of structured teaching offers students opportunities to assume the cognitive load while receiving support that helps them extend beyond what they could do alone. At the beginning of a lesson, the teacher explains, models, and demonstrates. Then with each phase of instruction, the cognitive load on the student progressively increases, with the teacher facilitating the work, stepping in and stepping away as needed. The framework has four phases (Fisher & Frey, 2008):

1 Focus lesson

2 Guided instruction

3 Productive group work

4 Independent learning

As we describe the gradual release of responsibility, we will explain and demonstrate how these practices are woven throughout a lesson or unit of study (all four phases may be part of a single lesson), and how they can be applied to instruction *of* English and instruction *in* English, as well as to instruction in the primary language.

Focus Lesson

As the name implies, this is the phase of instruction in which the teacher focuses the students' attention as he or she introduces the new learning. The purpose of the focus lesson is to build background knowledge, introduce new learning through direct explanation and modeling, and prepare the students for the upcoming task (Fisher, Frey, & Lapp, 2009). To this end, the teacher:

- Activates prior knowledge
- Establishes a clear purpose with high expectations
- Explains the concept, task, or skill
- Explicitly models his or her thinking and strategic use of metacognitive skills
- Demonstrates the expected product or behavior
- Focuses attention on target language and vocabulary

- Builds requisite background knowledge and vocabulary
- Provides examples and non-examples

This is the "I do it" phase, in which the teacher does almost all of the work. Modeling the strategies or processes serves to let the students see how an expert does it. As teachers, we have become so proficient in whatever it is that we're teaching that we do it without thinking. Often when we model, we show students how to do something as quickly as we would do it ourselves. But those who are new to using a strategy need to see the process in slow motion, demonstrated and explained. They need to see inside the teacher's thinking, to see and hear how an expert does it.

The focus lesson may be a shared reading and think-aloud in which the teacher models his or her thinking about a piece of text. It may be a science experiment in which the teacher models how to form a hypothesis, or a math lesson modeling how and why one estimates the answer to a problem. This phase is similar to when the baseball coach models how to throw a curve ball and explains when, how, and why the pitcher makes the decision to use it.

In our own practice, we have found that many English learners, especially those at early stages of language proficiency, benefit tremendously from modeling and, indeed, may need more modeling than native English-speaking students. Learning about new ideas in an unfamiliar language can take longer than when the learner already has the basic language and needs only the new ideas and technical vocabulary. When English learners don't have sufficient command of the instructional language to comprehend easily, they cannot rely on language or explanation alone. They may need multiple examples and demonstrations. Additional models can provide the redundancy of language so critical to language learning, giving these students more time to process the language, allowing them to hear the same idea expressed in different ways, and thus increasing their comprehension.

Guided Instruction

Sometimes called the "we do it" phase, guided instruction gives learners their first taste of assuming some of the cognitive load. Importantly, the teacher is there to provide scaffolds to support learning. These scaffolds come in three types: *questioning* to check for understanding; *prompts* to elicit background knowledge, activate procedural knowledge, or trigger metacognition; and *cues* to shift attention (Fisher & Frey, 2010).

When we think of guided instruction, we generally picture guided reading in an elementary school classroom, in which the teacher meets with a small group of students, all of whom have similar instructional needs in reading. This is one type of guided instruction; we can also provide small-group guided instruction in a content area, in language, or even in P.E. It is not always necessary to guide learning in a small group; it can be done with the whole class or individually as well. Having said that, there are advantages to small-group guided instruction for English learners, as these students are often the ones who sit quietly in whole-group activities, neither practicing language nor engaging in learning. It is far less intimidating for them to speak out in front of just a few other students.

Small-group guided instruction is based on needs identified through formal or informal assessments. It is not the same lesson for every group, and, importantly, the responsibility for learning is shared. That is, the students are not simply listening and watching, but they are doing—reading, writing, and practicing with content, language, or strategies. Perhaps the most important teacher behavior during guided instruction is questioning, as this provides formative assessment for further instruction. In addition, it is through asking the right questions that teachers guide students to think critically and construct their own meaning. Different students require different questions, depending on their level of understanding and what they already know and can do. One caution, however: all students need opportunities to respond to higher levels of questions that require critical thinking.

Productive Group Work

Productive group work, our term for what occurs during collaborative learning, is the next step in releasing an increasing amount of the responsibility for learning to the student (Frey, Fisher, & Everlove, 2009). Students receive less support and guidance from the teacher and jointly begin supporting and guiding their classmates, assisting one another in constructing meaning. This is the "you do it together" phase, in which the teacher is available for assistance, but the students are working together, sharing their ideas and learning, applying their learning, practicing key language and vocabulary, and extending their understanding of the concept or content.

We have come to call this phase of instruction productive group work because it describes what happens at this time: students collaborate to produce some type of product, such as a presentation, a piece of writing, or a summary, which gives them the opportunity to synthesize their learning in the company of peers. Though it is a group assignment, each student is required to show evidence of learning and his or her contribution to the product. This phase of instruction is often the noisiest, given the amount of student discussion that should be occurring. But appearances, as we know, can be deceiving, and this purposeful, productive noise serves as evidence of the students' growing command of the academic English they need in order to learn content. This phase is critical for English learners, as they need multiple opportunities to practice and use language. In classrooms where productive group work is not used, English learners may sit quietly most of the time and not produce—and thus not learn—language.

There are countless ways to provide opportunities for students to interact and talk, but the instructional routines that are most effective have certain characteristics in common. They are purposeful, structured, and hold all students accountable for the productive group work. The purpose of the interaction is clearly related to the purpose of the lesson. Students are familiar with the structure of the routine and have enough background knowledge to be able to complete the task with little assistance from the teacher. The assignments allow for multiple entry points, with tasks and resources differentiated to support every student's participation and learning. The routine is designed so the students' participation results in a deeper level of understanding.

The environment, physical and emotional, plays an important role as well. The room environment facilitates the interaction. Students feel supported and safe. They are willing to take risks, knowing their classmates will not ridicule them. Tables are arranged so that students sit in small groups or with partners and have ample space to create projects such as posters or triptychs. The furniture in the room facilitates flexible grouping, with tables and chairs easily moved to configure the room in different ways for different tasks. Resources are readily accessible; classroom walls are filled with models and charts that students can use to complete the task with their group, freeing the teacher to work with those who need more guided instruction.

Valuable as we recognize group work to be, it can be daunting for some teachers to take the first step in releasing control, trusting that students will stay on task and that they can and will learn without the teacher's telling them what they need to know. When students construct their own meaning with their peers, their learning may be deeper, longer lasting, and more generative than it is when they passively listen while the teacher talks. Of course, there are certain conditions that must be in place for this deeper learning to happen. Successful collaborative tasks do the following:

- Establish clear expectations and provide clear directions
- Provide academic challenge for all levels of students
- Relate directly to the purpose of the learning
- Offer language and content support along with differentiated resources
- Require all students to participate
- Follow established classroom norms for behavior
- Occur after students have sufficient knowledge of the content
- Take place in a supportive classroom environment
- Utilize familiar routines for collaboration
- Adhere to a specified and sufficient allotment of time (Fisher, Frey, & Rothenberg, 2008)

The teacher's role during the collaborative phase is to monitor and assess learning, forestall misconceptions, and assist various groups in clarifying understanding as needed. This can also be an opportune time to meet with a small group of students for additional guided instruction.

Independent Practice

The ultimate goal of our instruction is student independence ("you do it alone"). One common concern of teachers is that their students appear to understand the lesson and can produce competent work while the teacher is at their side, but then they are unable to demonstrate the same level of quality in their independent assignments. A primary reason for this disconnect is quite simple—the students do not yet have sufficient understanding or skill to complete the work independently. This does not necessarily mean that we need to repeat, review, simplify the assignment, or worse, lower our expectations. What it does mean is that we need to assess and analyze the students' learning, informally and formally. There may be just one piece that the student is missing. It is a fine balance to release the responsibility at the point where the student is ready for it—neither so soon that the student is not ready nor so late that the student is not challenged. This is the art and science of teaching. Art because we modify and adapt as we watch and listen to our students; science because we use ongoing assessment to inform these decisions.

Frequently we find that EL students lag behind the native English-speaking students in their readiness for independence. For a multitude of reasons, including unfamiliar language, unfamiliar content, or procedures and ideas that are unclear, English learners may need more teacher modeling and guided instruction, as well as more time to collaborate with peers, before they are ready to successfully do the work independently. In order to judge their readiness, we not only need to know our students' level of understanding, but we also need to be keenly aware of the language demands of the task and to identify the gaps between the language required and the language that our EL students can competently use. Armed with this knowledge, we can make choices about the additional instruction or scaffolding we can provide—support that will allow these students to demonstrate the same level of understanding as the native English-speaking students without being put at a disadvantage because of linguistic and cultural differences.

Three Essential Instructional Principles

In addition to a structured teaching framework that gradually releases cognitive responsibility to learners, three other essential principles are worth discussing, as they are necessary in order for English learners to excel. The first is establishing a clearly defined purpose, and the second is attending to the language demands of the discipline and the task. The third is teaching in a way that is culturally responsive, as this makes learning more effective and meaningful.

Clearly Defined Purpose

We know that English learners learn at an accelerated pace when they understand the purpose of the lesson (Hill & Flynn, 2006)—that is, what they will be expected to know and be able to do. A clear purpose also helps the teacher to remain focused, avoiding the trap of getting waylaid by too many "teachable moments" or activities and discussions that may be fun or interesting but do not serve the defined purpose.

Regardless of the subject matter, lessons should generally have a content purpose and a language purpose. We say "generally" because language lessons typically would have only a language purpose, utilizing familiar content to teach new language. In the content areas, each task requires specific language for understanding and for expressing that understanding. The language purpose addresses a specific language structure, vocabulary, or function and should require the use of each within multiple domains of language: listening, speaking, reading, and writing. Table 2.1 (page 32) provides examples of content and language purposes.

Language of the Content Area

We tend to think of mathematics as the subject easiest for English learners to access because it involves numbers, which are commonly understood in many cultures and languages. Math also often offers step-by-step visual support. However, many countries write numbers differently or teach different problem-solving methods, which can lead to student confusion.

As mathematics instruction focuses on understanding abstract concepts and not just on procedures or operations, it requires higher levels of language. In order to talk about even such concrete topics as geometrical figures, language learners must learn more than the names of the figures. They must also learn the words that express descriptions, relationships, and locations. They must learn words and phrases that native English speakers learn at a very young age—*round*, *line*, *next to*, *larger/smaller/longer than*, *it looks like*, *it has*, *different*, and *all*—as well as the content-specific words that all the students are learning, such as *polygon*, *segment*, *intersect*, and the like. Another hurdle for EL students is that many content areas use common words that they may have already learned, but now the words have completely different meanings—words like *table*, *cell*, *space*, *mean*, *sum* (which sounds like *some*), *plot*, *like*, and *figure*.

Table 2.1: Content and Language Purposes

Subject	Content Purpose (Students will learn to . . .)	Language Purpose (Students will learn to . . .)
Science	Understand the properties of liquids	Describe two properties of liquids using the frame "Two properties of _____ are _____ and _____."
English language arts	Identify the main idea for a given set of supplemental details in a single paragraph	Formulate a topic sentence in writing
English language arts	Use knowledge of text features to identify author's purpose	Discuss the author's purpose with a peer
Social studies	Differentiate between food production and consumption	Use technical vocabulary to discuss examples with group members
Mathematics	Identify ratios as relationships between two quantities	Use the correct mathematical terms to describe the type of ratio in a given problem

Does this mean that we should teach basic vocabulary during math or science or history? Not at all. It does mean, however, that we need to be aware of the language demands of the task, make students aware of this language (establish a language purpose), and provide scaffolds for English learners that enable them to understand and participate in the learning. Preteaching vocabulary, using nonlinguistic supports such as visuals and charts, and using linguistic supports such as word banks or sentence frames (see table 2.2) are all scaffolds that can ameliorate the cognitive burden of learning language and content simultaneously.

Culturally Responsive Teaching

While having an instructional model is important, it is not sufficient to provide quality instruction for English learners. Learners need a classroom that is culturally responsive. Gay (2000) describes culturally responsive teaching as utilizing teaching methodologies, curricular materials, and communication techniques that bridge home and school cultures. This demonstration of caring about the knowledge, customs, language, and social roles a child brings with her to the classroom has become a part of what is now defined as "good teaching" (Au, 2009, p. 179). However, it cannot be left to chance. While knowing a few words in a child's native language or being aware of holidays and foods is a start, it is not enough. Speaking frankly, we have been party over the years to many conversations between teachers who possess a level of

Table 2.2: Sentence Frames in Core Content Areas

Subject	Language Function	Sentence Frame
Mathematics: geometry	Compare and contrast	A _____ has more _____ than a _____. A _____ is like a _____ because _____.
Science: habitat	Cause and effect	Many animals cannot live in the desert because _____. Due to _____, _____.
Social studies: immigration	Describe events over time	During _____, many people _____. Early immigrants to the United States had to _____. Now immigrants must _____.
English: persuasive essay	Persuade readers	I agree that _____, a point that needs emphasizing since so many people believe that _____.

cultural awareness that stops at the classroom door. We recognize this when an educator remarks that a student is "lazy" because he doesn't volunteer answers or a "troublemaker" because he calls out without raising his hand. Otherwise sensitive administrators can also be guilty, as when they question whether parents care about education when they are noticeably absent from school events or don't assist their children with homework (Lapp, Fisher, Flood, & Moore, 2002; Peña, 2000). As Jones (2007) notes, "The American educational system was designed for students from two-parent nuclear families with middle class money and values, who came to school with all the necessary materials and preparation" (p. 14).

A culturally responsive teaching stance requires that the child see himself and others not only in the physical materials of the classroom, such as books, but also in the teacher's knowledge of and reference to the historical, social, political, and linguistic contributions of the child's home culture. For example, some students acquire a skewed perception of their home language, especially when it is a non-Western language. They mistakenly believe that their native language doesn't possess the same rigor as English. We know many secondary ESL teachers who explicitly use the grammatical and linguistic structures of their students' first language to make connections to English structures. This accomplishes two goals: activating background knowledge and demonstrating that *all* languages have structure, rules, and rigor.

In addition, the teacher holds high expectations for all students. Students learning English as a new language can and should be exposed to the same standards-based instruction as all learners. But it is done within a framework that allows for reciprocal learning between teacher and student. This means that a culturally responsive teacher knows that he cannot afford to merely transmit knowledge (which doesn't really work, anyway). He must join his students as a fellow learner. While he may be the science expert in the room, they are the experts regarding how the science they are learning relates to home and culture. A culturally responsive teacher makes sure that students have the opportunity to talk with him, and with their classmates, about both the content and the context of their learning. And with each of these interactions, he recognizes his continual transformation as an educator. After all, isn't this really what we mean when we tell our students we should all be lifelong learners?

Extended Core Programs for English Learners

Because English learners must develop their language proficiency in addition to learning the grade-level content, they need extended time in quality core programs to be successful. There are several ways that schools and districts can extend the core program for English learners. These options include English language development instruction at the elementary level and English as a second language elective classes at the secondary level. Saunders, Foorman, and Carlson (2006) found that English learners in elementary classrooms that had a separate ELD block had greater percentages of instructional time devoted to oral language and literacy activities than EL students in classrooms without a separate ELD block. Because these extra supports are made available to all English learners, not just those at risk for failure, they are still considered to be part of Tier 1, core instruction. Students who do not respond to this core instruction will also need supplemental and intensive interventions, but these have to be provided in addition to the core program, and extended core program, that all English learners already receive.

In elementary schools, an ELD block is commonly scheduled after lunch. This block occurs in addition to the quality core instruction students receive that focuses on the English language arts standards. The ELD block provides instruction about the English language to English learners at their level of proficiency. This instruction might be based on specific content, such as science, or might be more generically language and literature based. For example, at an elementary school in San Diego, students across a grade level are regrouped based on English proficiency levels. Each group consists of students with no more than a two-level difference. Commonly, students at levels 1 and 2 (beginner and early intermediate) work together, students at level 3 (intermediate) are grouped together, and students at levels 4 and 5 (early advanced and advanced) are grouped together. Students who have been reclassified can be grouped together so that the teacher can monitor their progress and provide extended core instruction. Students who are fluent or native speakers can be grouped together as well. Each teacher at the grade level designs a three-week-long unit of instruction that addresses specific language proficiency levels. One teacher might focus on science content, another on social studies content, and another on art. Every three weeks, students rotate to another teacher so that they have opportunities to explore each of these areas while receiving instruction in language development at their proficiency level.

At the middle and high school levels, English as a second language is offered as part of the students' core courses. ESL can also be extended in the form of elective classes before or after school in order to give English learners further opportunity to "catch up" to their native English-speaking peers. Typically, this additional time is offered to all English learners and should thus be considered an extended core opportunity rather than supplemental intervention. Students at beginning levels of proficiency in English require focused English instruction at their level, as do those at higher levels. Students at the intermediate level and above can benefit from enrolling in the grade-level English class with a parallel language-support class that continues the focus on language development.

It is important to note that the ESL class should not serve as a replacement for core English classes for students at intermediate levels of proficiency; neither should the core English classes replace ESL instruction. *All* English learners must receive focused English language development. Those at the intermediate levels *also* need access to grade-level English. Without both ESL and grade-level English, these students are not receiving the core instruction necessary to reach high levels of achievement and proficiency. In the language of RTI, this means that they do not have access to Tier 1 instruction or expanded core instruction, and instead the school is relying on a replacement class to address student needs (not intervention tailored to individual students). When schools do not provide students with access to core content and provide only ESL classes, ESL classrooms can become depositories for all at-risk EL students, regardless of their linguistic or academic needs (Cosentino de Cohen, Deterding, & Clewell, 2005). Conversely, when schools provide only core content classes without ESL instruction, they are not providing their EL students with the appropriate opportunities to learn.

Of course, there are a number of other ways for providing English language development instruction for students and extending their access to core instruction. In addition to ELD and ESL classes, some schools add after-school programs; others schedule intersession or summer school classes. These are valuable opportunities for English learners to access the core curriculum. Again, it is important to distinguish between these kinds of opportunities and supplemental interventions. Unless the supports are driven by assessments and involve significant small-group instruction led by highly qualified teachers, they are not supplemental interventions. Unfortunately, in some places, these programs are identified as supplemental intervention (Tier 2). As we will explore further in chapter 4, the classification of extended core programs as supplemental or intensive interventions is inappropriate, is inconsistent with the RTI model, and will not likely result in increased numbers of English learners reaching proficiency or becoming bilingual. That's not to say that these opportunities are unimportant; they're what ensure that the majority of students make progress. In other words, they're necessary, but not sufficient.

Using a Structured Teaching Framework With English Learners

The foundational elements of effective instruction, integrated with the gradual release of responsibility, can easily become part of any lesson or unit of study. With added attention to the instructional needs of English learners, this framework ensures that the vast majority of students benefit from quality core instruction.

Let's see how Yazmin's teacher uses the elements of effective instruction for English learners to teach a science unit on animal adaptation.

Clearly Defined Purpose and the Gradual Release of Responsibility

The purpose guides student learning in all four phases of the gradual release framework. We establish both the language purpose and the content purpose during the focus lesson. Students know and understand the purposes, and at the end of the lesson they reflect on their learning in relation to the purposes. The learning tasks throughout the structured teaching framework are clearly related to the purposes, serving to develop understanding of the content and proficiency in the language of that content.

Yazmin and her classmates in Ms. Ortiz's third-grade classroom are in the midst of a unit of study on adaptation. They are learning about how plants, animals, and humans have adapted to the environments they live in. They are now looking at how various animals have adapted to the extreme conditions in the desert. Ms. Ortiz makes sure that Yazmin and the other students understand the content and language purposes for the lesson (see table 2.3). She has posted them on the whiteboard and discusses them as well.

Table 2.3: Content and Language Purposes for Adaptation Lesson

Content Purpose (Students will learn to . . .)	Language Purpose (Students will learn to . . .)
Create an animal that could live in the desert	Use comparative language to describe how a desert animal is the same or different from other animals

Modeling and the Gradual Release of Responsibility

For the most part, modeling takes place during the focus lesson. However, it is not limited to that time. At any point in a lesson or unit, teachers may find that some students need additional modeling. The teacher may provide additional examples or different examples that connect more closely to the students' background knowledge and then spend more time showing the process or strategy to a small group or an individual student.

Using "I" statements, Ms. Ortiz shows the students how she goes about reading and understanding:

> The first thing I do when I read an article is look at the title and think what it might be about and what I already know about this subject. The title of this article is "Desert Jaws!" [Lambeth, 2008]. When I see this title, I think the article is going take place in the desert. I also think of the movie *Jaws*, so because I know that sharks are dangerous and bite, I think it will probably be some type of dangerous animal that bites.

Ms. Ortiz continues reading while the students watch her interact with the text, highlighting, circling, and making notes on the document camera. She chooses a passage that will allow her to model strategies for figuring out the meaning of a word she doesn't know:

> "Unlike a true scorpion, a wind scorpion has a hairy body and no stinger on the tail end. But it is related to true scorpions . . ." Now there's a word I don't know—*unlike*. But I know what *like* means. It's something that you like. And I know that *un* means *not*. So let me go back, substitute the words I know for the word I don't know, and then reread the sentence. "Something doesn't like a true scorpion, a wind scorpion has a hairy body . . ." Well, that can't be right, they're describing the scorpion. I must have the wrong meaning of *like*. Students, talk with your partner to see if you know another meaning of *like*, then put it together with *un* and be prepared to reread the sentence to the class with a different word for *unlike*.

Interaction and the Gradual Release of Responsibility

It's common sense that you can't learn a language unless you use the language. It stands to reason that this truism applies to virtually everything we do, whether it is cooking, riding a bike, skiing, or reading and writing. While it is not the only factor, we improve reading by reading. We improve writing by writing. And we improve our ability to speak another language by speaking that language. Research has shown that the active role of producing language fosters deeper, longer-lasting, and more fluent language (Swain, 1995). When students talk with their classmates about academic content, they expand their language, stretching their linguistic resources as they clarify, question, and contribute ideas. This interaction is one of the primary factors in developing both language proficiency and content knowledge. Students can be interacting and discussing at any point in a lesson, including the modeling and independent phases, but it is during productive group work that they have an extended period of time to talk about the content.

Ms. Ortiz has told her third-graders that they will create animals that are able to live in the unique and harsh environment of the desert. Students divide into expert groups to complete a jigsaw reading. Each expert group reads a different article on desert animals and their adaptation. These groups may be homogeneous when they are assigned to read a specific article at a specific reading level. Or they may be heterogeneous if they select the reading according to interest. Ms. Ortiz has grouped her students according to their English language proficiency so that she can differentiate text difficulty according to their reading and oral language skills. Yazmin's expert group discusses a reading on the Texas horned lizard and writes notes on a T-chart. On one side of the chart they note the characteristics of their animal; on the other they explain how each characteristic helps the animal to survive in the desert. They return to their heterogeneous home groups and now have experts on four different desert animals. In a Whip Around Share, one student at a time reads one characteristic at a time. Others in the group check it off if it is on their list or write it down if it's not. The next student repeats the characteristic and adds another one. They continue in this manner until they have each read all their characteristics.

Other supports include a word bank on the wall that Ms. Ortiz and the students have created as they have learned about the desert and its inhabitants. Ms. Ortiz has also provided some sentence frames to help the EL students express their ideas. All the students use them, though, because they still need the model of how to use more academic language than what they typically use in their conversations. Here are the frames for the adaptation lesson:

- One characteristic of a _____ is that it has _____.

- This helped the _____ adapt to the desert because it _____.

- One characteristic of a _____ is that it is able to _____.

- This helped the _____ adapt to the desert because it didn't have to/need _____.

Each student next selects at least one important characteristic that the group's creature will have or be able to do and draws a sketch of what that might look like. Individually the students also write statements explaining how the creature has adapted to the desert. They share their thinking, and then the group names the creature and selects a statement from the ones they wrote on their own or writes a new statement. Each group creates a poster showing the animal in its environment with the statement about its adaptation and a symbol that visually represents the concept of adaptation and will help them remember the meaning.

Guided Instruction and the Gradual Release of Responsibility

This is the time when the teacher meets with small groups of students who have similar needs. For example, some students need reteaching of certain concepts so that they don't fall too far behind. Other students need guided instruction to clear up misunderstandings and misconceptions. Students who already grasp the content might need guided instruction to push their thinking to higher levels of understanding. Guided instruction in Tier 1 is part of the differentiation and scaffolding that all teachers provide. When a student starts to fall further behind and the guided instruction given during core instruction is not sufficient to close the gap, the student will receive additional guided instruction in Tier 2.

Small groups provide a safe environment for EL students to participate in the classroom. They are more willing to risk making mistakes. They can take additional time to respond to a prompt, or they can offer a response using simple words. Using small-group instruction also helps to maintain an appropriate pace in the classroom because, rather than slow the lesson down to help an English learner with skills or knowledge that the other students already have, the teacher is differentiating her support. Small-group instruction is easiest to implement during either the collaborative or the independent phase of the lesson. While students work together or independently, the teacher can provide additional guided instruction for those who need a bit more support before they can successfully take on more of the cognitive load.

When the students go to their expert groups, Ms. Ortiz sits with a group of English learners whom she has purposefully brought together because they have similar proficiency levels in English—level 1 (beginning) and Yazmin's level 2 (early intermediate). Ms. Ortiz reviews the key vocabulary and checks for understanding of the big idea of adaptation. She then helps the students read the article as partners, stopping them and asking questions that require them to think about what they're reading, instead of simply word calling, as many students at this level tend to do.

Language Focus and the Gradual Release of Responsibility

There are many factors that affect reading comprehension, including language, vocabulary, background knowledge, text style, and student interest. Perhaps most important is the language of the text, which affects reading comprehension more than the student's background knowledge about the content (Goldenberg, 2008). When the text does not contain supports for comprehension, even students who have prior knowledge about a topic may be unable to make meaning. Supports such as redundancy, explanation and elaboration, examples, or transition words hold clues that help students follow the author's argument.

Previously we looked at establishing purpose and the importance of including a language purpose in our lessons. Simply having a language purpose and posting a few sentence frames on the board are not sufficient to teach the language students need. We must integrate explicit teaching of the language of text in the lesson, explaining and modeling how specific language constructs serve the specific purpose of expressing the content students are learning.

We often present the language focus during the focus lesson. Then we must maintain that focus throughout the unit of study. As we model reading a text or demonstrate a procedure, we model the language we want students to learn and use. We also call their attention to it so that they recognize it when we do it. Consider this situation. During ELD time, a teacher has been teaching his EL students to use irregular past tense with common words. A child arrives late to class one day. When the teacher asks her why she is late, she replies, "Mi mamá taked me to doctor." The teacher gently corrects the child by modeling the correct grammar: "Your mother *took* you to the doctor." The child nods her head, pleased that her teacher understood her English. But without a further cue that draws the child's attention to the error and the correction, the teachable moment vanishes. If we model language without making sure the students recognize what we're doing and why, we lose a valuable opportunity to help them develop proficiency.

Instruction that effectively fosters development of language proficiency has four essential characteristics—characteristics we have mentioned in other contexts in this book—that are present throughout all four phases of the gradual release of responsibility model:

1 Opportunities to interact with other students using the new language or vocabulary

2 Scaffolds that support students as they begin to try on new language

3 Situations that require authentic use of language

4 Expectation and accountability for using the language

We have seen Ms. Ortiz modeling how to determine the meaning of an unknown word during the focus lesson. She selected a word that can demonstrate more than one strategy. *Unlike* signals comparison, and it is a compound word that allows students to use what they know about a word to make meaning. During guided instruction, Ms. Ortiz maintains her focus on comparative language, asking one group to find words that signal comparison and giving another group sentence frames to help them find the comparison words. During the collaborative phase, she reminds the students that they are expected to use specific comparison language in their spoken language, on the poster, and during their presentation. She reminds them about the chart from a previous lesson on comparison words and sentence frames.

Meaningful and Challenging Tasks and the Gradual Release of Responsibility

Most of us are motivated to work at something when we have a good reason. We may have an interest in traveling, for example. We may have a need, such as learning a new online grading program that simplifies the process of calculating grades. And it's not so different in the classroom. Which would you rather do—answer every other question at the end of the chapter on the respiratory system, or create a travel brochure inviting visitors to take a cruise through the respiratory system, citing the highlights they will see along the way? Neither one is a particularly authentic task. In our lives, we don't write answers to a list of questions simply to show someone else our knowledge. Nor do we usually write travel brochures, though we may need to use those same persuasive skills to convince someone to do something.

It isn't always possible within the confines of the classroom walls to design tasks that one would actually do outside of them. However, the travel brochure task forces us to analyze the information, identify key points, and synthesize them to create an inviting picture. It challenges us to use higher-level thinking skills, and it taps into our creativity. It's also a task that allows for multiple entry points. All students can complete this task, regardless of whether they are advanced or still learning the content and language. We have all seen what can happen when students are asked to complete a task that is too difficult for them. At best, they simply don't do it. At worst, they disrupt the class. Similarly, when the task is too easy, students may be bored or finish early and then, with too much time on their hands, disrupt the class. And, sadly, we have wasted precious learning time. Designing meaningful and challenging tasks to move students to deeper learning is a challenging task in itself. At the same time, we realize how meaningful it is when we see the results.

Ideally, we would like all our tasks to be meaningful and challenging. The reality, however, is that sometimes students simply need to practice. Multiplication tables for instance, or sight words. For the most part, students can do this rote practice at home, independently. For most learning in the rest of the four phases of a structured teaching framework, tasks should be meaningful and challenging. In the focus lesson, we want to stimulate the students' interest and curiosity with meaningful models that students can connect to their own experience and knowledge. During guided instruction, the task should be challenging enough that students might need teacher guidance in order to complete it. When we design a task that requires students to work together to complete it, they are more likely to engage in productive group work.

And when the task is meaningful and poses the appropriate level of challenge, students are more likely to complete the independent work.

In order to create their own desert creatures, the students in Ms. Ortiz's class need to have a good understanding of the desert habitat and the ways in which various adaptations enable animals to survive there. At first glance, creating a creature may seem like merely a fun activity, but it is also an assignment with a high level of challenge. To provide differentiated support that students can access according to their need, Ms. Ortiz has built in many scaffolds:

- Background knowledge students have built through previous study of plants in the desert and habitats around the world

- Connections between the big idea of adaptation and the students' personal experiences of change and adaptation

- A variety of resources about the desert and its inhabitants, including texts and websites at different reading levels, models and visuals of animals in the desert, and stories of life in deserts around the world

- Resources that contextualize the learning, placing the big idea of adaptation into a larger and more concrete context

- A graphic organizer to organize students' thinking and learning

- Word banks and sentence frames that support the students as they talk about their learning

- Peer assistance

- Opportunities to discuss the content with their peers in their primary language

- Additional guided instruction for students at earlier levels of language proficiency or those who are having difficulty with the assignment

Metacognition and the Gradual Release of Responsibility

A primary factor in developing independence as a learner is the metacognitive process of thinking about and reflecting on learning. From their first days in school, students get accustomed to being told what to do and how to do it and being helped when they encounter difficulties. This is a large part of our role as teachers: organizing the students' school life, deciding what they must learn and how and when they will learn it, and telling them when they are ready to move on. It is no surprise, then, that many students remain dependent on our presence and assistance. Most teachers are good learners who automatically reflect on their learning, how they learned something, where they stand in relation to the goal, and what more they need in order to reach the goal. Yet we often focus so much on the content that students must learn and the instructional design of the lessons that we sometimes gloss over the importance of the students' role in evaluating their own learning. Students need to be very clear about what the goal is for the learning and then assess where they are in relation to that goal, reflect on what helped or hindered their learning, and identify what else might help them reach the goal. In order to become independent, students need to know what learning strategies help them personally complete various kinds of tasks, and then they need to consciously and purposefully implement them.

Metacognition is a part of every phase of the gradual release of responsibility. During the focus lesson, we model how we reflect on our own learning. We ask students to reflect after guided instruction. During the collaborative phase, we ask students to evaluate their product in relation to the standard, as well as to reflect on how the group helped them learn and on their own contribution to the group. When students begin their independent work, part of their task must be to plan what they will do to complete the assignment and how they will do it and then to review their work before they present it.

Throughout the lesson, Ms. Ortiz provides opportunities for her students to think about their learning. Before they begin to decide what characteristics their desert creature will have, she asks them to do a Think-Write-Pair-Share about *how* they will make this decision and *what resources* they can use to help them. After they have shared their individual ideas in their group, she asks the students to develop a work plan that includes an outline of what they will do to complete the project and that specifies what each group member will be responsible for. Yazmin has created work plans before, but if she needs a refresher, there is a chart on the wall with an example of a work plan. After the students create their poster, they judge it according to a rubric that sets the standards for the project. They rate it in each category and justify the rating. At the end of the lesson, Ms. Ortiz asks them reflective questions about their learning. The first question asks them to think about the essential question "Why do living things adapt?" The second question requires them to reflect on their work within the group. "How did the group help you work? How did you help the group?" Yazmin talks with her partner first and then writes her responses in her journal. A few students share out, telling the class something they heard their partner say.

Student Choice and the Gradual Release of Responsibility

On virtually any university campus at lunchtime, one will find an array of choices of food. This was not always so. At one time, dormitory menus offered an entrée, a side dish, and a dessert. If a student didn't like it, she'd buy a can of soup and heat it in her room or run across the street for a hamburger and fries. Then those in charge realized that students wanted choice in their meals. And so began a culinary revolution on college campuses around the country. We all like to have choices in our lives. Each of us has different interests and different talents from the person sitting next to us. Our students have these differences as well, and when we offer choices in assignments or resources, we not only honor their individuality and build on their strengths, but we also place more of the responsibility for learning on their shoulders and increase the likelihood of their success.

Giving students choices does not mean providing individualized assignments and resources for each student. Rather it means offering a menu of resources, projects, and assessments from which students can select those that best match their interests, skills, and learning styles. We can give students choices throughout all phases of the gradual release model, though it is perhaps most important to offer this menu during the independent phase. Allowing students to choose how they will demonstrate their learning enables us to gain a more accurate picture of what they learned. A song or poem about a mathematical procedure can demonstrate understanding every bit as well as a description or explanation of the steps. We can also offer students choices during guided instruction and productive group work, such as selecting the text they will read with the teacher or choosing the resources for the project they will complete during peer collaboration.

The students in Ms. Ortiz's class know that they can choose from among all the resources in the room about the desert. Some are using folktales to help them design their creature, while others use pictures or comparison charts. Each group also decides how it will present its creature. Ms. Ortiz gives the students a list of options for their presentation, including a poster, a wanted poster, or a letter home. If students have their own idea, she approves it, provided it is comprehensive, demands an appropriate level of rigor, and uses the academic language, written and oral, that they have learned in this unit. Yazmin's group wants to do a reader's theater for their presentation, and Ms. Ortiz makes certain that the group writes and rehearses adequately before the presentation.

A structured teaching framework featuring a gradual release of responsibility model of instruction provides numerous opportunities for English learners to practice language and improve their proficiency while also learning content. This framework can be strengthened when teachers differentiate their instruction based on the profiles of specific English learners.

Differentiation for English Learners in Tier 1

English learners are as diverse a group as any other students in our schools, and as such need different supports within Tier 1. Previously, we described four groups of English learners: recent arrivals with little literacy, recent arrivals with high literacy, students not yet proficient in English but progressing adequately, and long-term US residents making little or no progress in English. Tier 1 for each of these major groups of EL students provides different support. What this looks like will vary from district to district and from school to school, depending on the numbers of students, the available resources, and community input.

Recent arrivals with low literacy in their primary language and little or no English. These students need an intensive course in English that teaches "survival" language and lays a foundation of language and background knowledge for success in core subjects. When available, instruction or support in the primary language can help provide access to the core so that students are able to keep pace and learn grade-level content while they gain proficiency in English. It is not reasonable to expect that students, particularly at the secondary level, who do not speak English will comprehend even well-designed grade-level instruction in English until they have acquired some amount of English.

Recent arrivals with high literacy in their primary language and little or no English. These students also need an intensive course in English. The difference is that we can expect them to progress rapidly and be able to access grade-level instruction sooner than those with little literacy. Let us be clear that "sooner" does not necessarily mean after a few months. Since these students are schooled and literate in their primary language, they, too, will benefit from content-area instruction or support in that language, if available. Some students are highly skilled in a particular subject such as math or science and can often be successful in mainstream classes taught in English with some additional support. This additional support is still considered part of Tier 1, since students must receive the instruction needed to provide access to the core—the opportunity to learn—until and unless we determine they are not responding to instruction. And they still require focused English language development appropriate to their level of proficiency.

Students who have lived in the United States two to five years and are approaching native-like proficiency in English. Tier 1 for these students again must include English language development and support for learning grade-level content. There are a variety of ways to provide this support, such as a separate class, additional instruction, or a primary language aide. The critical components to providing the opportunity to learn are that we offer focused instruction in the English language and that we can ascertain that these students understand grade-level content and produce work that demonstrates that understanding.

Long-term US residents who have little literacy in their primary language, adequate oral communication in English, and poor academic literacy skills in both languages. These are the students who, for any number of reasons, have not had the opportunity to learn. They may not have had appropriate instruction in the English language. They may have experienced failure early on in their schooling and given up. They may have a learning disability, but this should not be the first option we consider. When we know that they have had access to the type of instruction we describe in this chapter, and they still do not respond, that is the point at which we assess further and discuss Tier 2 options. Unfortunately, it is often the case that these students have not had access to quality instruction and thus have not had the opportunity to learn for multiple years. The first step is to provide that quality instruction within Tier 1. The older the students are, however, the less likely it is that this will be sufficient to catch them up to grade level. Most of these students will probably require more intensive intervention than Tier 1 can provide. Thus, the current group of long-term EL students may move quickly into Tier 2.

The key to designing appropriate Tier 1 instruction is to know the students' strengths and needs and to be flexible in how we build on those strengths and meet those needs. Until we provide quality instruction *in* and *of* English, we will continue to grow large numbers of long-term English learners.

Quality Instruction for English Learners Versus Quality Instruction for All Learners

Effective Tier 1 instruction for English learners is not so very different from effective instruction for all learners. But it is different. It is not the same instruction that native English-speaking struggling readers and writers need. There are simply too many nuances and subtleties of language and culture that those who are new to the United States will miss. Native English-speaking students, even those who read well below grade level, will easily understand this excerpt of text:

> Rafael hopped on his bike and rode it down the street. When he got to his friend's house, he tossed a pebble at the window and shouted for him to come down. Both were looking forward to the game, but they knew it would be a close one.

The EL student, however, may be tripped up by the referential and possessive pronouns *his*, *it*, *he*, *him*, *they*, or the two uses of the word *down*, or the substitution of the word *one* for *game*, or the ellipsis *both*.

Clearly, all students benefit from the type of instruction described in this chapter. There are two major differences for English learners: the amount of support for both language and content, and the direct instruction *of* English.

SOLUTIONS FOR TEACHING ENGLISH LEARNERS

1. All staff members have a common understanding of and commitment to "opportunity to learn" for students from culturally and linguistically different backgrounds. We begin with awareness. We must be aware of ourselves as teachers and aware that English learners are different from native English-speaking students. From awareness, we must perceive the need for change.

We must recognize that students who are different need a different kind of instruction. From perceiving the need, we move to commitment. Change, by definition, upsets the order of things. Inadequate though the current order of things may be, it is familiar, and because it is familiar, we believe it to be easier. When we make a commitment to provide the opportunity to learn for all students, we are able to implement the changes and stick with them or adapt them until we know they work.

2. **English language development is part of the core for English learners.** This statement speaks for itself. When students don't speak English, they need to learn English. Therefore we need to provide the opportunity to learn English. We need to provide *quality* English language development for a long enough period of time that students become proficient in English.

3. **Sound core instruction is essential to supporting English learners.** Without quality core instruction that is responsive the needs of English learners, other efforts are diluted. It is shortsighted for schools to train their full attention on interventions without first considering the instructional environment of the classroom. That the instructional design of the class-room is sound is not a foregone conclusion. Our experience has been that most teachers have not spent time analyzing instructional design since their credentialing program. As novice educators, they were distracted by the initial management challenges that confront inexperienced teachers. An extended schoolwide focus on quality instruction is well worth the effort and helps the school prepare for students who do need more intensive intervention.

CHAPTER 3

Using Data to Rally Resources

LOOKING AT HER DATA CHART, middle school educator Ms. Jacobs wonders aloud, "I'm not sure what to make of this." The PLC meeting hasn't started yet, but Ms. Jacobs is clearly puzzled. She turns to Mr. Andrews, pointing to her data, and adds, "I have to go first."

When the grade-level meeting starts, Ms. Jacobs raises her hand. "I'd like to start. Okay with everyone?" Her peers nod in agreement, and Ms. Jacobs continues. "When I screened their writing, several of my students had big-time spelling problems. It seemed like half the class needed Tier 2 intervention. But now look at the data. They're getting it! I only have a couple of students who need that level of support anymore. The rest are doing fine, so I can focus on other things now."

Mr. Andrews, congratulating Ms. Jacobs on her data, asks, "So, what happened? Why'd it work so well this year?"

Ms. Jacobs, pausing to give this some thought, finally answers, "I guess it's because I asked for help earlier this year. The screening data really alarmed me, so I went right to Ms. Sawyer [reading specialist] and Ms. Armento [bilingual special educator] and begged them to spend every minute they could in my room. Together, we went after the needs. And it's working! I'm really proud of my kids."

Ms. Armento agrees and adds, "It's been great to be in your room so much. I really feel like I'm part of the team. I get to meet with students on my caseload and provide a few incidental benefits for students in need. But I am still worried about a few students, including Eduardo, who doesn't seem to be making much progress yet."

Ms. Fernandez, another member of the grade-level team, asks what they plan to do about Eduardo. "He's really a great guy, but I'm worried that he'll just get passed along like it seems other schools have done. He really needs more supplemental instruction. Can we take a look at his screening measures again?"

Ms. Sawyer flips on her computer and soon has Eduardo's screening assessment displayed on the smart board. Ms. Fernandez addresses Ms. Jacobs: "So you're attacking the spelling, right? Who's working on his writing? Has he made any progress there? It's important that we're not just looking at spelling, but really his overall ability to communicate in writing."

Ms. Armento joins the conversation again, indicating that she's been working on his writing and has administered a number of writing assessments to determine his strengths and needs. "I think I've got that covered, but can I report back on him at our next meeting? I want to do a writing sample assessment that's analytic, so I can focus on syntax and semantics. It's a bit more detailed than the holistic writing rubric we use for the seventh grade." The team agrees and Ms. Fernandez says, "Perfect. We have a plan and we'll meet up again soon."

The teachers in this school use their grade-level PLC meeting time to focus on student learning. As part of their conversations, they use assessment data to determine the success of Tier 1—core instruction—and make recommendations regarding students who might need supplemental interventions, or Tier 2 supports. Importantly, they talk with one another about their students and make decisions together about how to affect student achievement. RTI provides teachers with a purpose for having these conversations rather than assuming that every teacher is an independent contractor who has all of the answers, resources, and skills to meet the needs of all of the students in the class.

Between Tier 1 and Tier 2 Lie Assessments

As part of quality core instruction, teachers routinely check for understanding. They can do so through oral language interactions and questions, as well as by assigning written products, projects, or tests (Fisher & Frey, 2007). In addition to using a variety of formative assessments to check for understanding, teachers use them to plan instruction (Moss & Brookhart, 2009). These are routines that have a strong evidence base and are expected to be part of the work every classroom teacher does.

RTI takes assessment further. While instruction is critical for RTI to work, assessments are the driver of the system. Assessments allow teachers to determine student needs as well as student progress. Assessments, it has been said, distinguish between teaching and learning. When learning does not occur, teachers have to take action. That action, in an RTI system, is supplemental intervention. That's why we think of assessment data as the link between Tier 1 and Tier 2 interventions, and why we have this chapter situated squarely between the chapters on quality core instruction and supplemental intervention.

The Difference Between Measuring and Assessing

We've used the term *assessment* intentionally. In some places, we have seen the measurement aspect of RTI increasingly emphasized, to the point that it has overtaken the instructional purposes of the approach. To borrow an expression used in New Zealand, where sheep outnumber humans: "You can't fatten sheep by weighing them." Likewise, measuring students is not the same as teaching them. If RTI devolves into another means for further categorizing students and does not result in very real instructional changes, then we're spending a whole lot of time and money with little to show for it.

An overemphasis on measurement also detracts from the teacher's expertise. A system that values the measure at the expense of the teacher puts money, time, and effort only into training teachers how to administer and score the instrument, rather than into developing their skills for the teaching that should take place as a *result* of the measurement. When measurement is valued over instruction, "the valued expertise is the design and selection of tests that can be used by people with limited expertise, and [of] packaged, often scripted, intervention programs" (Johnston, 2010, p. 602).

As do the International Reading Association and many other organizations, we view assessment as a means for determining which children need more attention, and as a method for determining whether an intervention is working *for a specific child*. Not every intervention is useful for every child. However, an RTI approach that values measurement blames the child; one that values instruction recognizes that initial and ongoing assessments provide insight into whether the intervention needs to be refined (Johnston, 2010). The International Reading Association (2010) has published a brochure called "Response to Intervention: Guiding Principles for Educators," which can be downloaded from its website, www.reading.org.

Professional development on assessment is necessary and valuable when it is coupled with analyzing assessment results for the purpose of future instruction. Both the means of assessment and the instruction need to be culturally responsive to magnify a student's strengths and not just focus on deficits (Orosco & Klingner, 2010). When it comes to English learners, assessment is likely to be far less uniform than a simple measurement system that values consistency above all else. For this reason, assessment tools must be chosen based on the needs of the learner and the teacher. Some of the most valuable assessment instruments are ones that are locally developed (at the grade, school, or district level) to reflect the community, culture, expectations, and standards. That's why curriculum-based measures, which will be discussed later in this chapter, are so useful.

Tier 2 supplemental intervention, then, is based on student performance. Teachers design supplemental intervention based on what students know and still need to know. To determine which students need supplemental interventions, two categories of assessments are used: screening tools and progress-monitoring tools. Given our focus on English learners, we will describe some specific tools that are useful for this population. We assume that all students, including English learners, are also being assessed with more generic screening and progress-monitoring tools. The generic literacy tools we often see in schools include assessments

such as Dynamic Indicators of Basic Early Literacy Skills, or DIBELS (dibels
.uoregon.edu); Developmental Reading Assessment, or DRA (Beavers, 1999); and
the Gates–MacGinitie Reading Test (www.riverpub.com/products/gmrt/index
.html). While these tools are useful in many situations, English learners often
require other assessment approaches that focus on their language and literacy
development.

Screening Tools

Regular screening measures are necessary for the effective implementation
of RTI for English learners. Screening tools should identify students who
are at risk of experiencing difficulty. Most schools already use a number of
screening tools. We can all remember parading through the nurse's office to
have our hearing or vision checked. Covering one's eye and reading letters
from a chart wasn't something to be embarrassed about; everyone was assessed
with this tool.

Like vision and hearing screening tools, the screening measures used in
RTI efforts are easy to administer and result in the identification of students
who *might* need intervention. But while national comparisons work quite
well for measures of eyesight or hearing, measures of language skills need to
be calibrated with an appropriate reference group. For English learners, the
comparison should be twofold. Before a school recommends intervention, an
individual student should be compared with true peers, meaning students who
are also learning English and who have similar language experiences (Brown
& Doolittle, 2008). English learners should also be compared with native
speakers, but a gap between these two groups may or may not necessitate
supplemental intervention. If a specific student is making progress as expected,
intervention is probably not necessary.

In general, schoolwide screening should occur in conjunction with progress
monitoring. Whereas vision and hearing can be reasonably assessed less often,

> school-wide screening is conducted to identify a subset of stu-
> dents whose response to Tier 1 general education is then moni-
> tored for a relatively short period of time to (dis)confirm the risk
> status indicated via school-wide screening. Only the subset of
> students who (a) first meet the school-wide screening cut point
> and (b) then evidence poor rates of improvement over five to eight
> weeks of Tier 1 general education are deemed in need of a preven-
> tative intervention.
>
> Our recommendation is that schools use school-wide screening in
> combination with at least five weeks of weekly progress monitor-
> ing [of] response to general education to identify students who
> require preventative intervention. Our rationale is that one-time

universal screening at the beginning of the year can over-identify
students who require preventative intervention. (Fuchs & Fuchs,
2006, pp. 39–40)

For example, at Seyo's school, all primary students participate in a DIBELS universal screening during the first two weeks of school so that teachers can get initial information on students who may be struggling with beginning reading skills. Seyo's first-grade teacher, Ms. Sanchez, learns that the girl has regressed since the last benchmark at the end of her kindergarten year. This isn't unusual among young children, but Seyo's teacher is further concerned that the girl's status as an English learner places her at increased risk. She makes a note to follow up with further assessment information to gain a fuller understanding of Seyo's language and literacy development. In addition, Ms. Sanchez will engage in progress monitoring over the next few weeks to see if being back in the classroom after the summer break will jumpstart Seyo's reading acquisition.

In terms of English learners, there are a number of specific tools that teachers and schools can use to screen students and then monitor their progress early in the school year. School teams should work together to agree on the screening tools that they will use. This provides teachers an opportunity to discuss results and interventions as part of their professional learning communities work and to set expectations for the school overall as part of a continuous improvement effort. Table 3.1 (page 54) is a task list for selecting and using screening tools. While this is a generic tool, we have found it very helpful in guiding discussions about appropriate tools for English learners. Next, we'll review four different examples of screening tools that are useful for teaching English learners.

Checklists

Checklists provide teachers with a list of intended behaviors or skills against which student performance is evaluated. Checklists are often less detailed in explaining traits and expectations than are rubrics. They are often designed by groups of teachers working with their grade-level or course-alike peers. For example, a group of high school English teachers developed a checklist to screen their English learners for possible writing difficulties. They were looking for specific things that students at the ninth-grade level should have already mastered. A few items from their checklist included:

- *Writing speed*—The student writes words on the page at a rate of at least thirty words per minute.

- *Spelling*—High-frequency words are spelled correctly.

- *Verb tense*—The student uses past-tense verbs correctly.

- *Agreement*—Writing includes subject-verb agreement.

Table 3.1: Essential Task List for Selecting and Using Screening Tools

Directions: In the second column, write the name(s) of the individual or team who will assume responsibility for the task identified in the first column. In the third column, write the
deadline for or status of the task.

Task	Responsible Individual/Team	Timeline/Status
Review your screening instrument's items to be certain that content is aligned with the curriculum for each grade level.		
Once a tool has been selected, determine and secure the resources required to implement it.		
Determine initial professional development needs and continuing professional development support.		
Administer the screening measure three times a year (for example, early fall, midterm, and late spring).		
Create a database that aligns with the screening instrument to hold student information and scores.		
Organize the screening results (for example, graphs and tables) to provide a profile of all students and their comparisons with one another.		
Monitor results at the classroom level and make decisions about when teachers/instructional programs require more scrutiny and support.		
Add screening results to a database so that students' performance can be monitored over time.		
Specify written steps to follow when further scrutiny is needed for students judged to be at risk.		

Source: Johnson, E., Mellard, D. F., Fuchs, D., & McKnight, M. A. (2006). Used with permission.

- *Vocabulary*—Word choices suggest middle school or higher content knowledge.

In some cases, districts or state departments of education develop screening tools for English learners that schools can use. For example, the Oklahoma State Department of Education developed a screening tool for use with English learners just entering the school system at the prekindergarten level (see fig. 3.1). Tools such as this one are helpful in generating a list of names of students for whom progress monitoring should begin immediately. These tools are also useful for calibrating expectations, especially when groups of teachers meet to review the assumptions and criteria they find in the checklists.

Sandy Garrett
State Superintendent of Public Instruction
Oklahoma State Department of Education

PRE-KINDERGARTEN LANGUAGE SCREENING TOOL
FOR ENGLISH LANGUAGE LEARNERS AND BILINGUAL STUDENTS

Directions: The initial portion of this screening can be performed in an informal format, such as when you are walking down the hall towards the office or as you greet the child; or, in a more structured format, seated at the table in a testing situation. To decrease anxiety on the part of the child and parent, it is suggested to use the informal format when possible. **If the child fails to answer the first three questions in English, discontinue the test.** If the child is unresponsive due to fear or reservation, the test can be performed after a few weeks into the school year.

	Yes	No
1. **What is your name**? *The child should be able to say at least their first name, and possibly their last name.*		
2. **How old are you**? *The child should state their age. If they only show their fingers to identify their age, ask "**How many is that**?"*		
3. **What are your favorite toys**? *The child should be able to list at least two or three of their favorite toys. If they need prodding, you can ask:* "**What do you like to play with at home**?" Or, "**What do you like to play with outside**?" *If the child fails to answer the first three questions in English, discontinue the test.*		
4. **Tell me about your** _____ (use one of the toys he/she mentioned). **What is it like**? *The child should be able to give you 2 or 3 characteristics about the toy.*		
5. **What are some of your favorite animals**? *The child should be able to name 3-5 animals.*		
6. Can the child follow simple directions such as: "**Put the pencil on the table**." "**Put the book under the table**." *Include prepositional words such as on and under.*		
7. Point to the child's eyes, ears, nose, hair, legs, arms, hands, feet, fingers, knees, head, or toes and ask "**What is this**?" *Can the child name at least 6-8 of them?*		
8. Ask the child to draw a picture for you. When the child is finished, say "**Tell me about your picture**." *If child needs encouragement, you can say:* "**Tell me about this part of your picture**."		
9. *When the child talks about their picture, does the child include endings on their words such as* **s**, **ed**, *or* **ing** *as in the words: playing, balls, rolled?*		
10. *Does the child use complete sentences with at least 3 or 4 words?*		

Total the number of items you answered "yes"... _____

Total the number of items you answered "no"... _____

Scoring instructions: Proficiency is 70% or 7 out of 10 items. For students who are unable to answer 7 of the 10 questions, they qualify for ELL services and qualify for "bilingual count". If you discontinued the test after the first three items because of incorrect responses, the child qualifies for ELL services.

March 2006

Source: Oklahoma State Department of Education. Used with permission.

Figure 3.1: Sample screening checklist.

Oral Language Observation

Given that most native speakers of English have sophisticated oral language development, it is rare to find schools and districts that routinely screen for oral language. But in an RTI system focused on English learners, teachers are wise to notice English learners' oral language development. As Britton noted, "Writing floats on a sea of talk" (1983, p. 11). There is plenty of evidence that this is the case (for example, Dockrell, Lindsay, & Connelly, 2009). It's clear that print-based communication systems are built on oral language structures (Wolf, 2007). For English learners, oral language development is critical if we expect them to become readers and writers (Winsor, 2007).

The tool we use most often for screening oral language development is the Student Oral Language Observation Matrix, or SOLOM. The SOLOM is an informal screening tool that has proven useful in helping teachers judge oral language proficiency within a school setting (Peregoy & Boyle, 1997). It can be used to determine a student's English acquisition phase, to identify student needs, and to record the progress of individuals and groups. It is appropriate for both the elementary and secondary levels because it is not based on developmental milestones.

The SOLOM allows teachers to rate students on five key dimensions of oral language: comprehension, fluency, vocabulary, pronunciation, and grammar. Each of these five dimensions may be rated on a scale from 1 to 5, yielding a total score range of 5 to 25 (see table 3.2, pages 58–59). To administer the SOLOM, the teacher observes students in several different classroom activities in which they are interacting with the teacher and/or their classmates, such as cooperative group tasks. On each occasion, the teacher marks rankings on the matrix according to his or her impressions of the student's use of English. Some teachers audio-record one or more of the sessions to review and confirm impressions or to examine patterns of errors or usage. To increase validity, teachers should use the SOLOM only with students they have been teaching for at least a month. They can also cross-check ratings from the different contexts in which the child is observed for consistencies or for variations that may indicate different levels of proficiency for different language functions or purposes. The SOLOM yields scores that correspond to four phases of English language proficiency:

- Phase 1 = Score 5–11
- Phase 2 = Score 12–18
- Phase 3 = Score 19–24
- Phase 4 = Score 25

The SOLOM is useful for several reasons, including:

- Focusing teachers on language development goals

- Highlighting students' progress in oral language development
- Reminding teachers to provide oral language development activities so that students have opportunities to progress in their speaking, and thus reading and writing, skills

But most importantly, the SOLOM identifies areas of instructional need. Mr. Jimenez, Eduardo's physical education teacher, used the results from the SOLOM screening tool to identify areas of the student's language development that could be addressed during sports. Eduardo scored a total of 13 points on the SOLOM, placing him in the early production stage of English language acquisition. His strengths are fluency, vocabulary, and pronunciation; he scored a 3 on each of these three traits. He is very quiet and is very shy about speaking English. His vocabulary is developing, but he limits his speech to only specific words. Teachers can understand him if they listen very closely, and usually after he repeats himself. His weaknesses are comprehension and grammar. He understands only a small portion of what is said to him. When he speaks, his grammar is not correct, and it causes his words to lose meaning.

Here's what Mr. Jimenez reports at the PLC meeting. The team listens as he describes what he has done to develop Eduardo's language:

> I have approached him when he was with a small group of peers while doing an activity. Academically, Eduardo is doing okay in physical education because I teach by doing demonstrations. He may not always understand what I am saying, but he still understands what he is supposed to do. Socially, he is doing well. He has made a lot of friends in the class, and they interact well, both in Spanish and English. Since all except two students speak Spanish in my class, Eduardo is able to communicate with the other students.
>
> Since comprehension was one of his weaknesses, I have been spending more time with Eduardo either alone or in a small group. After I demonstrate or model what the students are going to do for the day, I ask him to retell me the instructions in English. Of course, I let him check in with other members of the group in Spanish if he wants. Then we review the events in English. I provide some scaffolds for him and repeat things back to him when he makes mistakes. I also notice every time he uses past tense incorrectly, and we fix that. It's the part of grammar that he and I work on together.

Just think of the impact that this type of supplemental intervention—additional small-group instruction focused on specific needs—could have on Eduardo and students like him if every teacher used screening results to support language development.

Table 3.2: Student Oral Language Observation Matrix

Based on your observation, mark an "X" across the block in each category that best describes the English learner's abilities.

Trait	1	2	3	4	5
Comprehension	Student cannot be said to understand even simple conversation.	Student has difficulty understanding what is said; comprehends only social conversation that is spoken slowly with frequent repetitions.	Student understands most of what is said at slower-than-normal speed with repetitions.	Student understands nearly everything at normal speed, although occasional repetition may be necessary.	Student understands everyday conversation and normal classroom discussions without difficulty.
Fluency	Student's speech is so halting and fragmentary as to make conversation virtually impossible.	Student is usually hesitant; often forced into silence by language limitations.	Student's speech in everyday conversation and classroom discussion is frequently disrupted by the student's search for the correct manner of expression.	Student's speech in everyday conversation is generally fluent, with occasional lapses as student searches for the correct manner of expression.	Student's speech in everyday conversation and classroom discussions is fluent and effortless, approximating that of a native speaker.
Vocabulary	Vocabulary limitations are so extreme as to make conversation virtually impossible.	Student misuses words and has very limited vocabulary; comprehension is quite difficult.	Student frequently uses wrong words; conversation is somewhat limited because of inadequate vocabulary.	Student occasionally uses inappropriate terms and/or must rephrase ideas because of lexical inadequacies.	Student's use of vocabulary and idioms approximates that of a native speaker.

Pronunciation	Pronunciation problems are so severe as to make speech virtually unintelligible.	Student is very hard to understand because of pronunciation problems; must frequently repeat what is said in order to make him- or herself understood.	Pronunciation problems necessitate concentration on the part of the listener and occasionally lead to misunderstanding.	Student is always intelligible, though one is conscious of a definite accent and occasional inappropriate intonation patterns.	Student's pronunciation and intonation approximate those of a native speaker.
Grammar	Errors in grammar and word order are so severe as to make speech virtually unintelligible.	Grammatical and word-order errors make comprehension difficult. Student must often rephrase what has been said or restrict him- or herself to basic patterns.	Student makes frequent grammatical and word-order errors that occasionally obscure meaning.	Student occasionally makes grammatical and/or word-order errors that do not obscure meaning.	Grammatical usage and word order approximate those of a native speaker.

Written Language Observation

English learners should also be screened for written language development. While there are a number of screening tools that are useful for gauging writing development, the Student Written Language Observation Matrix, or SWLOM, was created by the California Department of Education specifically for EL students. Like the previous assessment, it can be used at the elementary or secondary level. Scores on the SWLOM are slightly different from those on the SOLOM, given that there are six dimensions of writing, each of which is to be evaluated on a scale of 1 to 4, yielding a total score range of 6 to 24 (see table 3.3).

The SWLOM score ranges that correspond to the four phases of language proficiency are:

- Phase 1: Score 6–10
- Phase 2: Score 11–15
- Phase 3: Score 16–19
- Phase 4: Score 20+

Like the SOLOM, the SWLOM provides teachers with general guidelines for instructional interventions. As is common with many English learners, Eduardo's writing scores were lower than his oral language scores. His proficiency, in terms of writing, was 12. He scored a 2 on each of the six factors, suggesting that all areas of writing needed to be addressed. In this case, his teachers realized that he needed more diagnostic assessments to determine areas for intervention. His teachers also knew that they needed to monitor his progress, or else he'd end up another year older with no more skills than he started the school year with.

W-APT

The final screening tool we'll review was published by the World-Class Instructional Design and Assessment consortium, a group of experts on English learners whose mission is "to promote educational equity and academic achievement for linguistically and culturally diverse students through the development and dissemination of curricular, instructional, and assessment products and resources" (Wisconsin Center for Education Research, 2007). The W-APT, which stands for the WIDA-ACCESS Placement Test™, is a screening tool used by educators to measure the English language proficiency of students who have recently arrived in the United States or in a particular district. It can help to determine whether or not a child is in need of English language instructional services, and if so, at what level. This tool has to be purchased from WIDA directly, so we won't say much more here other than to note that screening tools specific to the needs of English EL students are difficult to find, and good ones are worth their weight in gold.

Table 3.3: Student Written Language Observation Matrix

Based on your observation, mark an "X" across the block in each category that best describes the English learner's abilities.

Trait	1	2	3	4
Fluency	Writes single words with no sentence structure	Writes short sentences with limited sentence structure	Writes complete sentences with developmental sentence structure	Writes paragraphs with fully developed sentence structure
Organization	No logical sequence or organization	Lacks logical sequence and organization, but the writer has attempted a sequence or an organization	Somewhat sequenced to substantially sequenced	Follows standard organization for the genre
Grammar	No grammatical relationships	Basic word-order problems, uses only present-tense form	Minor grammatical errors	Grammar resembles that of native speaker of same age
Vocabulary	Insufficient vocabulary to express ideas	Limited vocabulary, relies on first language for translation	Knows most words, but lacks vocabulary for finer shades of meaning	Flexible in word choice, similar to native speaker
Genre	No concept of form	Does not differentiate form to suit purpose	Chooses form to suit purpose but limited in choice of forms	Knows different genres and makes appropriate choices
Sentence variety	No sentence pattern	Uses one or two sentence patterns	Uses several sentence patterns	Uses a full variety of sentence patterns appropriately

Universal screening instruments are useful and necessary as the first line in identifying students who might need a closer look. We think of these instruments as a means for putting students on our radar. However, these screening instruments are a snapshot in time and give us only a static image of who that student is. To extend the metaphor further, progress monitoring introduces movement. Just as a photograph is different from a video, progress monitoring gives us a way of viewing the student across a period of time.

Progress Monitoring

As we have noted in the discussion of screening tools, progress monitoring is an important part of the RTI system. The assessments used as part of progress monitoring help teachers determine if students are benefiting from classroom instruction and interventions. As with screening tools, there are a number of more generic tools available for all students. Information about progress monitoring is rapidly expanding. The National Center on Student Progress Monitoring, sponsored by the US Office of Special Education Programs, provides an array of free, Web-based progress-monitoring resource materials at www.studentprogress.org. The National Association of State Directors of Special Education (NASDSE, 2005) identified nine essential characteristics for progress monitoring in an RTI system. Progress monitoring should do the following:

- Assess the specific skills embodied in state and local academic standards

- Assess marker variables that have been demonstrated to lead to the ultimate instructional target

- Be sensitive to small increments of growth over time

- Be administered efficiently over short periods

- Be administered repeatedly (using multiple forms)

- Result in data that can be summarized in teacher-friendly data displays

- Be comparable across students

- Be applicable for monitoring an individual student's progress over time

- Be relevant to development of instructional strategies and use of appropriate curriculum that addresses the area of need (pp. 25-26)

While not specifically developed for English learners, these nine features of progress monitoring are important considerations in the development and implementation of tools designed to guide instruction and intervention for students learning English.

Progress monitoring serves different functions, based on which tier of the system we're talking about. For Tier 1, quality core instruction, progress monitoring indicates whether or not students are progressing as expected. The data provide information about the impact that instruction is having on students. Again, if fewer than 70 to 80 percent of the students are reaching the expected levels of achievement on these assessments, the focus should be on improving the quality of the core instruction. At the classroom level, grade level, or subject-area level, data can be aggregated to evaluate the success of the overall curriculum and suggest areas of change or improvement. These data can also be used to determine whether the rate of growth in a given area will be sufficient to ensure that grade-level expectations are met. At the individual student level, progress-monitoring data can be used as part of Tier 1 to determine which students require supplemental (Tier 2) or intensive (Tier 3) interventions.

The issue of cut points can be a tricky one, especially as it applies to English learners. As we noted earlier in this chapter, it is important for students learning English to be compared to true peers (those with similar proficiency levels and experiences), as opposed to only native English speakers. For this reason, schools and districts may identify cut points on progress-monitoring tools that are designed for English learners to help teams of teachers make decisions about which students might require intervention. In other cases, a particular commercial instrument may be normed and therefore have set cut points in place. When assessing English learners, it is necessary to look at the description of the normative group to determine whether the cut points are useful or not. If the normed group is very different from the student, then the results should be considered with that caveat in mind. Schools may want to identify alternative cut points for EL students or use the assessment for information gathering rather than for placement purposes.

A second issue that applies to cut points on assessments is the overall purpose of a response to intervention system. One that is constructed primarily with measurement in mind is likely to place more importance on the over/under factor. On the other hand, one that is developed with instruction and intervention in mind recognizes that the trajectory (growth over time) is far more informative than the static (moment in time) image of a child's performance relative to the cut point.

In a responsive RTI system, progress monitoring is used to determine whether or not the intervention is helpful. As part of their progress-monitoring work, schools and districts need to make decisions about discontinuing supplemental and intensive interventions based on the evidence collected or when to make a formal referral to special education. A team task list for Tier 1 progress monitoring is presented in table 3.4 (page 64), and one for Tier 2 progress monitoring is presented in table 3.5 (page 65).

Curriculum-Based Measures

One of the most common ways to monitor progress is to use curriculum-based measures (CBMs). The work on CBM began in the mid-1970s with research headed by Stan Deno. Over several years, curriculum-based

Table 3.4: Essential Task List for Progress Monitoring in Tier 1

Directions: In the second column, write the name(s) of the individual or team who will assume responsibility for the task identified in the first column. In the third column, write the deadline for or status of the task.

Task	Responsible Individual/Team	Timeline/Status
Within the relevant content area, review the progress monitoring measure or tool selected for Tier 1 to determine whether content is aligned with your curriculum.		
Once a tool has been selected, determine and secure the resources required to implement it (e.g., computers, folders/copies, testing areas).		
Determine initial professional development needs and continuing professional development support.		
Implement a system of data collection and progress monitoring that includes determining both level and growth rate.		
Administer the progress monitoring measure frequently enough to assess a learner's responsiveness. At Tier 1, screening is three times a year, with routine monitoring weekly or twice weekly.		
Monitor results at the individual student level and make decisions about reasonable cut scores to determine movement to Tier 2 and beyond.		
Monitor results at the classroom level and make decisions about when teachers or instructional programs require more scrutiny and support.		

Source: Johnson, E., Mellard, D. F., Fuchs, D., & McKnight, M. A. (2006). Used with permission.

Table 3.5: Essential Task List for Progress Monitoring in Tiers 2 and 3

Directions: In the second column, write the name(s) of the individual or team who will assume responsibility for the task identified in the first column. In the third column, write the deadline for or status of the task.

Task	Responsible Individual/Team	Timeline/Status
Implement a system of data collection and progress monitoring that includes determining both level and growth rate.		
Within the relevant area of focus for the intervention, review the progress monitoring measure or tool selected for Tier 2 and beyond to determine whether content is aligned with the intervention.		
Administer the progress monitoring measure frequently enough to assess a learner's responsiveness. At Tier 2, two to five times per week is the research-based recommendation.		
Organize results to provide a profile of the student's progress within this tier. This could be a graph of test scores supplemented with student work samples.		
Monitor results to determine whether a student is responding to the intervention.		
Develop decision rules about when to return a student to Tier 1, when to continue with Tier 2 and beyond, and whether further scrutiny of student performance for special education is warranted.		

Source: Johnson, E., Mellard, D. F., Fuchs, D., & McKnight, M. A. (2006). Used with permission.

measurement systems were developed in reading, writing, and spelling (Deno, 1985). Deno's work on CBMs is a foundational premise of RTI and has been utilized for decades, particularly in special education. Ideally, CBMs should:

- Be easy to create
- Be quick to administer and score
- Have acceptable levels of reliability and validity
- Provide a variety of forms that allow assessment data to be collected over time

An online generator for CBMs can be found at Intervention Central, a free website containing resources for response to intervention measures (www .interventioncentral.org). At this point, we will highlight a few measures that have been useful in progress monitoring specifically for English learners. Of course, there are a host of generic progress-monitoring tools that teachers can also use and that are available at Intervention Central's website.

Oral Reading Fluency

An effective way to monitor progress, and one that has significant cross-over effects from native speakers of English to English learners, is to administer periodic assessments of students' oral reading. It seems that oral reading ability is correlated with overall reading ability, both for English learners and for native speakers (Hasbrouck, 2006). Hasbrouck and Tindal (2006) identified norms for oral reading fluency, which can be found in table 3.6.

Oral reading measures are fairly easy to conduct. First, the teacher selects a reading passage. This can be either a commercially available grade-level passage or a passage from the student's reading curriculum. The student reads the passage aloud for one minute while the teacher identifies the number of words read correctly. When using this procedure for screening, the teacher selects passages from text at the student's grade level. When using it as part of progress monitoring, the teacher selects passages at a student's individually determined goal level. For example, if a fifth-grade student is at a third-grade instructional level, the teacher may use passages at the fourth-grade level for progress monitoring.

When a student is significantly below the national norms and his or her language peers, supplemental intervention is probably warranted. If the student is making progress and perhaps outpacing his or her language peers, the core instruction is probably working, and the student does not need supplemental intervention. What to do when an English learner requires supplemental or intensive intervention is the focus of the next two chapters. For now, we'll maintain our focus on progress-monitoring tools.

Table 3.6: Oral Reading Fluency Norms, Grades 1–8

Grade	Percentile	Fall WCPM*	Winter WCPM*	Spring WCPM*	Avg. Weekly Improvement**
1	90		81	111	1.9
	75		47	82	2.2
	50		**23**	**53**	**1.9**
	25		12	28	1.0
	10		6	15	0.6
2	90	106	125	142	1.1
	75	79	100	117	1.2
	50	**51**	**72**	**89**	**1.2**
	25	25	42	61	1.1
	10	11	18	31	0.6
3	90	128	146	162	1.1
	75	99	120	137	1.2
	50	**71**	**92**	**107**	**1.1**
	25	44	62	78	1.1
	10	21	36	48	0.8
4	90	145	166	180	1.1
	75	119	139	152	1.0
	50	**94**	**112**	**123**	**0.9**
	25	68	87	98	0.9
	10	45	61	72	0.8
5	90	166	182	194	0.9
	75	139	156	168	0.9
	50	**110**	**127**	**139**	**0.9**
	25	85	99	109	0.8
	10	61	74	83	0.7
6	90	177	195	204	0.8
	75	153	167	177	0.8
	50	**127**	**140**	**150**	**0.7**
	25	98	111	122	0.8
	10	68	82	93	0.8
7	90	180	195	202	0.7
	75	156	165	177	0.7
	50	**128**	**136**	**150**	**0.7**
	25	102	109	123	0.7
	10	79	88	98	0.6
8	90	185	199	199	0.4
	75	161	177	177	0.5
	50	**133**	**151**	**151**	**0.6**
	25	106	124	124	0.6
	10	77	97	97	0.6

* WCPM = Words Correct Per Minute   **Average words per week growth

Source: Hasbrouck, J., & Tindal, G. (2006, April). Oral reading fluency norms: A valuable assessment tool for reading teachers. The Reading Teacher, 59(7), 636–644. Used with permission of the International Reading Association. www.reading.org

Maze

The maze assessment is also fairly easy to conduct, in part because it is in written form and can be used with several students simultaneously, thus reducing the amount of time spent in assessment. It consists of selected passages in which words are periodically deleted (usually every seventh word) and replaced with three word choices, only one of which fits in the sentence (Wiley & Deno, 2005). One of the incorrect choices is a near distractor, meaning that it preserves the syntax, but not the meaning, of the sentence. The other incorrect choice is a far distractor, meaning that it does not make sense syntactically or semantically (Shinn & Shinn, 2002). Typically, the first sentence is left intact, and then targeted words are selected for use in the assessment. During the assessment, the student reads the passage silently and circles the word that best fits each sentence. The score is the number of correct selections in a given amount of time, typically three minutes. The passage should be between 150 and 400 words in length, to provide students with plenty to read during the three minutes and several opportunities to make their selections.

It is important to keep in mind that this is a progress-monitoring tool, and as such it is often used for looking at growth over time. Typically, the results are scored based on the number of words correct, followed by a slash, and then the number of incorrect words (Shinn & Shinn, 2002). The scoring is done only up until the last circled word; the teacher should not count the sentences that have not been completed because the student did not read that far.

For example, Ms. Sanchez used a series of maze assessments for several weeks with Seyo to see if she made gains during the six weeks of school. Her progress-monitoring results were as follows:

- September 14: 0/2 (Seyo made 0 correct selections and 2 incorrect ones.)
- September 22: 1/2
- September 28: 1/1
- October 7: 0/3
- October 13: 1/2

Given these results, Ms. Sanchez saw a pattern of high rates of inaccuracy and little growth, despite core instruction in the classroom. She knew that this wasn't the only measure she should rely on in making a decision about whether Seyo should participate in supplemental instruction, but the results did confirm what she was noticing in her classroom observations.

The maze tool has been used with native English speakers as well as English learners. Fuchs and Fuchs (1992) suggest that teachers may prefer the maze assessment over oral reading fluency measures because it requires both accurate decoding and comprehension. While most CBMs are useful for elementary school students, and especially students who speak English, maze has been shown to be useful in progress monitoring with middle and high school English learners as well (McMaster, Wayman, & Cao, 2006).

Eduardo's teachers have found maze assessments to be especially useful in their progress monitoring. At one point in the year, Eduardo's English teacher created a maze assessment from the text *Coraline* (Gaiman, 2002). She decided to use this text as many of the students in the class had seen the movie and were interested in the content. Using the maze generator at Intervention Central, Ms. Jacobs created a few different versions of the assessment. For Eduardo and a few other students, the maze focused on a basic list of common English words. For other students, Ms. Jacobs allowed the computer program to randomly select words to replace. And for other students, she purposefully replaced specific words with vocabulary words they had been studying over the past month. An excerpt of the version created for Eduardo, from page 40 of *Coraline*, follows. According to the Flesch-Kincaid scale, this passage was at grade level 4.3, meaning that seventh-grader Eduardo should have chosen the majority of the words correctly based on readability. He missed only one of the words from this passage, and Ms. Jacobs couldn't wait to share this success with her colleagues. That's not to say that Eduardo understood all of the words in the passage but rather that he understood the common English words and was using context clues to make predictions about which words should be in the selected sentences. Ms. Jacobs noted that Eduardo was ready for a new type of maze passage, one in which content-area vocabulary words were replaced.

> He picked up the flashlight in his mouth and trotted off into the dark. Coraline followed him. When he got **(flew, near, lately)** the front of the stage he **(stopped, torn, hospital)** and shone the flashlight onto an **(east, empty, mine)** seat. Coraline sat down, and the **(often, dog, expansion)** wandered off. As her eyes got **(used, leaf, during)** to the darkness she realized that **(the, bright, rejoice)** other inhabitants of the seats were **(also, button, regularly)** dogs. There was a sudden hissing **(key, ice, noise)** from behind the stage. Coraline decided **(glove, it, building)** was the sound of a scratchy **(destruction, agreeable, old)** record being put into a record **(goat, player, hole)**. The hissing sound became the noise **(make, of, fragile)** trumpets, and Miss Spink and Miss Forcible came onto the stage.

Running Record

For the youngest students who are just beginning to read and understand connected text, ongoing assessment is vital. The running record, developed by Clay (2006), is part of a six-part assessment of early literacy behavior. The running record is one portion that can be administered repeatedly, as per NASDSE guidelines, as it is really a system for coding errors and corrections as the child reads a short book or passage. The teacher codes the child's oral reading performance and later analyzes errors and corrections to look for patterns in the types of mistakes being made (see table 3.7). The purpose is to hypothesize what cueing systems—graphophonic, syntactic, and semantic—the student is using and not using as he or she makes a particular error or correction.

Table 3.7: Coding Conventions for the Running Record

Reading Behavior	Convention
Accurate reading	✓
Repetition	R
Self-correction	SC
Teacher cues to "Try that again"	TTA
Pauses	P
Substitution	[write word]
Omission	_____
Insertion	^
Child appeals/teacher tells	A/T
Spells or makes individual sounds	Cat/c-a-t

The usefulness of this form of data collection is that it can be done with any book or passage. In addition, it provides timely information about the match between text difficulty and the reader, as well as insight into what the child is relying upon as he or she reads. Text difficulty is measured post hoc as the percentage of words read correctly (the number of words read correctly, divided by the total number of words in a passage):

- Independent level: 95%–100%
- Instructional level: 90%–94%
- Frustration level: ≤ 89%

The data collection and the analysis of text difficulty allow the teacher to continually calibrate the choice of books during Tier 1 core instruction or Tier 2 supplemental intervention. In addition, the use of this information makes instruction more responsive to the individual needs of the student, as the teacher can design lessons to address the errors that were uncovered in the process. The running record, like all assessments, should not be used as a single-event measure. Instead, the reliability of this approach increases significantly when at least three running records on a student are collected, and when two educators examine the results (Fawson, Ludlow, & Reutzel, 2006).

Informal Reading Inventory

While running records are useful for beginning readers, they do have limitations in both scope and practicality. The running record does not focus on comprehension, and therefore a child could correctly read a story while still possessing relatively little understanding of the overall text. In addition, students who have moved beyond the beginning reading stage tend to read more rapidly, making coding more difficult.

An informal reading inventory is an assessment consisting of leveled text passages and word lists that provide a comprehensive look at a reader's current strengths and areas of need. There are many of these tools available, but we favor the *Qualitative Reading Inventory-4* (QRI-4, Leslie & Caldwell, 2005). In addition to word lists and leveled narrative and expository passages, the QRI-4 features comprehension questions before and after the reading and a student think-aloud scoring protocol for use with older readers. In addition, this inventory offers extensive technical information regarding its interrater reliability (the likelihood that two people would score a reading event similarly) and its content validity (the likelihood that the instrument measures what it says it is measuring). The QRI-4 is a technically reliable and valid measure of reading ability through high school and thus meets the NASDSE recommendations for using sound measures that relate to state standards.

Analytic Writing Analysis

Measures of writing performance are useful because they access another language domain that is essential to success, both inside of school and out. Unfortunately, many of the holistic writing rubrics commonly used in classrooms and schools, while useful for teaching, do not have the technical qualities that are needed for progress monitoring. In a study comparing curriculum-based measures of writing and a holistic writing rubric, the CBMs were found to correlate strongly with standardized writing measures, while holistic measures did not (Gansle, VanDerHayden, Resetar, & Williams, 2006). Similar findings have been reported for high school writing (Diercks-Gransee, Weissenburger, Johnson, & Christensen, 2009). Curriculum-based measures of writing typically give students a brief amount of time (six to ten minutes) to produce a sample that is long enough to analyze. The sample is then analyzed for the following features:

- Total words written (TWW)
- Average number of words written per minute (AWPM)
- Total words spelled correctly (TWSC)

- Total number of complete sentences (TCS)
- Average length of complete sentences (ALCS)
- Correct punctuation marks (CPM)
- Correct word sequences (CWS)
- Incorrect word sequences (ICWS)

Most of these indicators are self-explanatory, but word sequences deserve further elaboration. A word sequence is two adjacent words in a sentence that should be spelled and capitalized correctly and make sense within the context of the writing (Videen, Deno, & Marston, 1982). On paper, a correct sequence is indicated by an upward-facing caret (^), and an incorrect one is marked with a downward-facing caret below the sentence line ($_\vee$). When a sentence begins with a reasonable word, that word counts as a correct sequence; the same holds true when the last word of a sentence is considered reasonable. The tool we use for analyzing writing samples is shown in figure 3.2.

Now let's look at writing samples from two of the students featured in this book. Third-grade student Yazmin was asked to write to the following story starter and given six minutes to complete her piece: *Describe your favorite room in your house. Tell what is in there and why it is your favorite. Use the descriptive language we have been studying.* Here is her sample, as marked by the teacher:

> ^My^bathroom^is$_\vee$ovor$_\vee$the^house^. ^My^dog$_\vee$in$_\vee$kitchen^. ^I^am$_\vee$
> sleep^in$_\vee$bedroom^. ^My^sister$_\vee$watch$_\vee$his$_\vee$oclock$_\vee$. ^I^play$_\vee$my^friend^.

An analysis of her writing shows the following:

1 Total words written (TWW): 24
2 Average number of words written per minute (AWPM): 4
3 Total words spelled correctly (TWSC): 21
4 Total number of complete sentences (TCS): 5
5 Average length of complete sentences (ALCS): 4.8
6 Correct punctuation marks (CPM): 5/5
7 Correct word sequences (CWS): 18
8 Incorrect word sequences (ICWS): 11
9 CWS – ICWS = 7

The results indicate that Yazmin's overall writing fluency is low, averaging only four words per minute, and her sentences are equally short in length, demonstrating a lack of descriptive language or complex sentence structures. Yazmin uses punctuation correctly, although it is notable that her sentences needed only periods. She begins all sentences with a capital letter, and she spells 87.5 percent of the words correctly. However, the relation of correct to incorrect word sequences is 7, indicating that there are a number of errors of language, syntax, or vocabulary that warrant further instruction.

Student: _____ Grade: _____ Age: _____	
Date of Sample: _____ Start time: _____ End Time: _____	
Administered by: _____ Analyzed by: _____	

What direction or prompt was given to the student?	
Did the student need encourage-ment to continue? Explain.	
What are your overall impressions of the writing sample as it relates to content accuracy and adherence to the prompt or direction?	

Please attach the writing sample to this document.

Total words written (TWW) _____

Average number of words written per minute (AWPM) _____

Total words spelled correctly (TWSC) _____

Total number of complete sentences (TCS) _____

Average length of complete sentences (ALCS) _____

Correct punctuation marks (CPM) _____

Correct word sequences (CWS) _____

Incorrect word sequences (ICWS) _____

CWS – ICWS = _____

Figure 3.2: Analytic writing analysis tool.

Seventh-grade student Eduardo completed a thirty-minute timed writing sample in his English class, for which students were given the following directions: *Write a persuasive essay. Choose a topic you care about, and tell why the reader should do as you say. Include a counterargument.* Here is his sample, as marked by the teacher. Underscores indicate incomplete sentences.

> ^You^should^wear^a^helmet^because∨You∨fall^you^could^break^ your^head^. ^It^is^for^your∨safty∨. ^It^could^help^you^live^. <u>You^ ride^your^bike^and∨hit^by^a^car^, you^could^be^o.k.^but∨you^ land^on^your^head^and^crack^it^open</u>∨.
>
> ^Your^parents^and^family^would^have^trouble^living^because^ you∨have died∨for∨not^wearing^a∨helment∨ when^you^are^on^ your^bike^

^Your^bike^and^you^could˅damage˅. ^You probly˅kill^someone^ else^because^they^could˅drive˅the^car^and turn^when^you^fall^ and^they ^might^hit^something^. ^You^could^die^for˅alots˅ of^ reasons^when˅your˅not^wearing^ your^helmet^when˅your˅riding^ your^bike^.

^I^think^it˅save^your^life^if^you^land^on^your^head^when^you^ ride^a^bike^.

An analysis of this passage shows the following:

1 Total words written (TWW): 129
2 Average number of words written per minute (AWPM): 4.3
3 Total words spelled correctly (TWSC): 124
4 Total number of complete sentences (TCS): 7
5 Average length of complete sentences (ALCS): 14.6
6 Correct punctuation marks (CPM): 10/11
7 Correct word sequences (CWS): 112
8 Incorrect word sequences (ICWS): 24
9 CWS – ICWS = 88

As did Yazmin, Eduardo has a very low overall word-production rate, suggesting that writing fluency is of significant concern. Unlike Yazmin, he has several fragmented sentences, although the average length of his complete sentences (14.6) suggests that he is using more complex structures, such as dependent clauses. His overall rate of punctuation is good, as is the number of words he spells correctly. However, he also has a relatively high number of incorrect word sequences. The errors he makes are most often grammatical ones, suggesting that he does not have full control of the syntax of the English language.

For students such as Yazmin and Eduardo, a curriculum-based measure of their writing can be used to monitor their progress and serve as a means for planning Tier 2 interventions for them. Both students struggle with writing fluency, a marker for writing production and complexity. As the next several weeks progress, their teachers will collect further information about their writing skills and make decisions about the need for possible Tier 2 supplemental intervention.

Standards-Aligned Checklists

Just as checklists can be used for screening, they can be developed as progress-monitoring tools for state standards. One method of creating a checklist for progress monitoring is to identify benchmarks based on proficiency levels for specific standards. As an example, Louisiana has the following English language development standard: *Students read, comprehend, analyze, and respond to a range of materials using various strategies for different purposes.* A progress-monitoring checklist that is used by the Rapides Parish Schools (2010) includes the proficiency levels for this standard and a benchmark for each level. Students at what is designated as Proficiency Level III are expected to "understand descriptive materials within familiar contexts and some complex narratives. The students use visual and contextual cues to derive meaning from text that contains unfamiliar words and expressions." The benchmark for this proficiency level is to "understand a more complex narrative and descriptive materials within a familiar context to continue to access the curriculum in core subject areas." To help students reach this benchmark, teachers would monitor their progress—several times a year until mastery—on the following skills:

- Demonstrate knowledge of taught contractions.
- Recognize common abbreviations.
- Use capitalization and punctuation to comprehend.
- Locate the meanings, pronunciations and derivations of unfamiliar words using dictionaries, glossaries, and other sources.
- Recognize and use knowledge of spelling patterns when reading.
- Recognize the format of poetry versus prose.
- Identify the main idea.
- Identify multi-syllabic words by using common syllable patterns. (Rapides Parish Schools, 2010)

Using this kind of progress-monitoring tool provides teachers with specific information about specific students and their instructional needs. If some of the students do not make progress, the teacher will need to consider supplemental interventions. As we will discuss further in the next chapter, if four students fail to recognize poetry versus prose after quality core instruction, the teacher will need to focus additional instructional intervention on that area of the curriculum.

SOLUTIONS FOR TEACHING ENGLISH LEARNERS

1. English learners should participate in the screening procedures used for all students, and special attention should be given to selecting tools that focus on aspects of language proficiency. Many of the screening tools that schools use can reveal important information about students. They are especially valuable as a means for alerting educators to learners who may have possible academic difficulties. However, screening procedures must also include tools that are informative for language proficiency and development.

2. Take "true peers" into account when analyzing assessment data. A true peer is an English learner at a similar level of proficiency, not a native English speaker. We should remember to take true peers into consideration when looking at normed data on these screening tools so that we can make meaningful judgments about the skills of English learners. We should keep in mind that learning English is not a disability and that language development happens over the course of a number of years. That's why progress monitoring is so important—we are looking for steady improvement. A positive trajectory with an adequate slope is indication that Tier 1 supports are working. An inadequate trajectory indicates that Tier 2 supplemental intervention is warranted.

3. Talk with other teachers about assessment results and their implications for instruction and intervention. For too long, teachers have closed their classroom doors and done their own thing. RTI is an invitation to change that. Teachers should bring their screening and progress-monitoring data to professional learning community meetings for discussion. When teachers work together in these learning environments, they contribute ideas for instruction, collaborate on interventions, and share in the successes and challenges that come with teaching all students at high levels.

4. Keep the purpose of initial screening and progress monitoring in mind. The overall intent of using such instruments is not to merely measure students but to use the results to plan instruction and refine it to make it more effective for the individual student. Therefore, teachers perform screening assessments to initially identify students who may need further instruction and intervention. They use progress monitoring to gauge the extent to which the instruction is working for the learner and to decide when it needs to be changed.

CHAPTER 4

Tier 2: Supplemental Interventions That Build Language and Content Knowledge

NINTH-GRADE STUDENT MINH rushes to her next class. It's English with Ms. McLean, and even though the content of the course stresses her quite a bit, she knows she also benefits from the extra support she receives. Minh has made limited progress in her English language proficiency, and despite being in US schools for seven years, she is still at level 3 (intermediate or developing), according to her eighth-grade state language assessment. However, Minh is at a new school that has a strong RTI component that is used to address the needs of its many English learners.

Mihn's English teacher has organized a unit of instruction on the essential question "Does age matter?" Every day the class listens to a passage from the target text, *Peter Pan* (Barrie, 1902/2003), and Ms. McLean uses this to teach lessons on literary devices. In addition, all the students in the class select related books from an extensive list of novels and informational texts about young and old characters facing challenges. Ms. McLean explains that this approach allows her to differentiate instruction (Tier 1) to accommodate student interests, background knowledge, and reading levels. Minh has chosen *Hattie Big Sky* (Larson, 2006) because, as she shares, "I like story about girls who must live alone in strange place." Minh and several other students who are reading the same book meet three times a week to discuss the text, and sometimes the English teacher joins their group.

However, Minh also needs further support, and so she meets twice a week with several other English learners and Ms. McLean. As part of this supplemental intervention (Tier 2), Ms. McLean previews passages from *Peter Pan* that she'll be reading later in the week with the whole class. She and the students examine the vocabulary and talk about the literary devices the English teacher will be highlighting. On this day, she draws their attention to the device of the kite that the main character uses to travel. As she asks them a question, she draws a kite to ensure they know the term. "Why do you think a kite is important in this scene?" she begins. The group engages in a lively discussion of a kite as a toy for little kids, and Minh queries, "Is it important that the kite is flying thing?" Ms. McLean nods in agreement. "Do you remember the term for that?" she asks, and gestures to the poster of literary devices she has displayed in the classroom. Minh furrows her brow in concentration and scans the list, then brightens. "A symbol!" she says, and Ms. McLean expands Minh's response as she writes it on a chart. "The kite is a symbolic device because it . . ." She pauses, and another student finishes the sentence. "Because it shows Peter's need to be free," he says. For the next several minutes, the group explores this idea, and Ms. McLean records their ideas on chart paper for them. As the discussion draws to a close, Ms. McLean asks them to record the chart in their literary notebooks so that they will recall their ideas and the terminology that they used today.

Ms. McLean later explains that she has several English learners who benefit from her frontloading (preteaching) the vocabulary that they will need in future readings. "I find that they are much more likely to participate when I do this," she says. "It gives them a chance to link together the technical vocabulary, like *symbolism,* with evidence from the text. We'll go further in our class discussion, but this gives them a leg up because they have seen a portion of the text and have pulled out an idea or two already. Not bad results for a fifteen-minute conversation."

Minh is fortunate that she is now attending a school that is focused on her development as a student and has implemented a system for monitoring her progress and providing interventions to assist her. While the school does identify several students a year for special education services, the real focus is on ramping up the language and literacy skills of the school's English learners. Minh was given several screening assessments during the opening week of the school year, when all students participate in a variety of assessments to guide initial placement and instruction. English learners are given several additional screenings so that their teachers can have up-to-date information on their English proficiency. Minh was struggling to keep up in most of her classes, so in the sixth week of the school year, she began participating in Tier 2 supplemental intervention. Ms. McLean also collaborates with a special educator and a language specialist as part of the school's professional learning community, and with their help she has implemented several practices to deliver Tier 2 supports in her classroom. In addition, the language specialist provides consulting services to Minh's other teachers so that they can implement supplemental interventions in their classes.

In this chapter, we will examine the instructional, curricular, and assessment implications of providing the Tier 2 supplemental interventions that some English learners need in order to make progress and close the achievement gap. We will end the chapter as we have previous ones, focusing on solutions that make RTI for English learners a reality.

Defining Tier 2, Supplemental Interventions

A response to intervention model consists of several layers of support, and these layers are multidimensional in terms of curriculum, instruction, and assessment. Tier 2 is the next avenue of intervention for students who are not responding to quality classroom instruction (Tier 1). There is often a "double dose" effect in Tier 2, as students are likely to participate in lessons that are linked to the classroom curriculum. General purposes for Tier 2 interventions include building background knowledge, frontloading content in advance of whole-class instruction, reteaching concepts that were not learned during initial instruction, and collecting assessment information to measure progress and inform instruction. For English learners, Tier 2 interventions may also be used for the purpose of developing language that is specific to upcoming lessons or building background about culture.

The structure and size of the group are important at this level. Tier 2 supplemental interventions are most commonly offered within the classroom in small groups of two to five students. Students are grouped based on an assessed need and may be regrouped depending on the focus of the lesson. This has implications for English learners in particular, as the stage of language proficiency alone is inadequate for grouping in Tier 2. While language proficiency information is valuable and a necessary element for a student's assessment profile, it is simply too broad to stand alone as a means for grouping. Instead, students are grouped according to instructional needs. For instance, the students Ms. McLean had placed in Minh's group in the opening scenario shared a need to preview complex readings so that they could more fully engage in critical analysis with the whole class.

Assessment is another hallmark of Tier 2 supplemental interventions. Information about a student's current learning is collected several times per month but should be collected more frequently as needed. These minimum recommendations are primarily for progress-monitoring purposes; it is likely that more frequent assessment is needed to plan instruction. In addition, progress-monitoring assessments come from the guided instruction that occurs in the group, especially in the form of questioning to check for understanding. We will discuss effective guided instruction later in this chapter.

Who leads the group depends on the focus of instruction. In many cases it is the classroom teacher, who is the natural choice for ensuring that supplemental instruction is linked to the classroom curriculum. In other cases, it may be a bilingual specialist, a reading coach, a special educator, or a provider of another related service (such as the speech/language therapist) who offers supplemental intervention in the classroom. We will voice a strong note of caution against using a paraprofessional, volunteer, or peer tutor for Tier 2 intervention. We have great respect for the work that all of these people do in schools and recognize that our classrooms would be poorer without them. However, a Tier 2 intervention group requires more expertise, not less. Instead of asking them to provide supplemental interventions, we should consider ways in which paraprofessionals, volunteers, and peer tutors can work with the students in the class who do not need supplemental instruction and intervention.

Another consideration in implementing Tier 2 support is the frequency with which the group meets, and for what period of time. Although this varies somewhat, the general consensus is that the group sessions occur three to four times a week, with each one lasting about thirty minutes. A number of other factors need to be considered, including developmental ones related to the child and how long he or she can be expected to attend to the task, as well as the extent of other supplemental instruction. Minh is a case in point. As a secondary student, Minh has several teachers each day, and concentrating all of her Tier 2 supplemental instruction within one course would not be feasible. Instead, her school's RTI plan for her specifies that she have similar sessions in several courses where the reading and vocabulary demand is high. As part of her supplemental intervention, Minh meets with her science and history teachers to preview readings. Because the duration of Tier 2 supports is typically nine to eighteen weeks, her teachers' PLC group is planning on providing this level of intervention for the first marking period of her ninth-grade year and will reevaluate based on her progress.

Taken together, the elements of Tier 2 supplemental intervention provide teachers and schools with a number of variables to manipulate as they support English learners in making progress. To summarize, these variables include the group size and composition, the number and types of assessments, the personnel who are leading the group, and the length and duration of the supplemental intervention. Making decisions about all of these requires a careful analysis of the role of assessment in RTI.

Grouping in Tier 2 Intervention

Because Tier 2 intervention is delivered to a small, need-based group of students, a closer look at grouping considerations is warranted.

How Big Should It Be?

As noted earlier, an intervention group generally consists of between two and five students. Bluntly stated, it is unlikely that the proper level of intensity can be offered in a whole-class setting of twenty to thirty-six students. We say this because it has become popular in some schools to simply relabel existing practices, such as English language development time, as a supplemental intervention. The practice of redistributing students by language proficiency levels across a grade level for more whole-class instruction, while building on the core program, simply does not offer the intensity required of supplemental interventions. This practice may be sufficient for students who are making progress in Tier 1; the focus of this chapter is on students who are not. Therefore, we can't in good conscience advocate for renaming an existing practice that doesn't result in anything different for the student in question.

Instead, we are talking about assembling students with similar needs for very focused guided instructional time. The first consideration is keeping the size of the group manageable so that the teacher can provide sufficient attention to each student. There is obviously good logic involved in this—after all, a teacher's attention is divided across the number of students he or she is working with. There is research on this as well. While there isn't a consensus on the "ideal" group size, one study on English learners is instructive. Vaughn and Linan-Thompson (2003) examined the effect of group size across a supplemental reading intervention for second-grade struggling readers. They used three different group size configurations: 1:1, 1:3, and 1:10. They found (not surprisingly) that students in the individual (1:1) and small-group (1:3) configurations outperformed those in the larger-group (1:10) format. They did not find a statistically significant difference in this reading program between the individual and small-group configurations.

Another factor to consider in determining group size is the relative differences among students. It is a truism that students at grade level are more similar than different and that their progress trajectory is more aligned with expected results, particularly those based on normed data. However, students who are struggling academically more often than not present a profile of scattered skills, with patterns of strengths and areas of need that are unique to the individual learners. Thus, although a group of students may cluster together when using one measure (say, language proficiency), they are usually different from one another on other measures. Therefore, even among a group of students gathered together to participate in a supplemental intervention, a group that is too large will tax the attention and skills of the teacher as he or she attempts to support each member differently.

What Gets Taught?

In addition to keeping the group to a manageable size, the teacher should select students based on instructional needs. When students are grouped in this way, the teacher is able to tailor lessons to specific groups. A non-example of a Tier 2 intervention is the teacher delivering the same lesson four times to four different groups of students. While she may be utilizing a small-group arrangement in order to deliver a lesson, the uniformity from group to group does not meet the standard of a Tier 2 intervention. Alternatively, consider Minh's teacher, Ms. McLean. In addition to meeting with Minh's group, which was described earlier, she meets with another small group of three students in her class who are well below grade level as measured by the school's screening test. The school's reading coach did informal reading inventories with these three students and developed a plan to support their reading growth. Ms. McLean meets with this small group three times a week while the rest of the class is meeting in literature circles to discuss their books. Her group focuses on problem-solving strategies to increase reading comprehension. The focus of this work is very different from that of the work she does with Minh's group.

When Can This Happen?

Because Tier 2 interventions usually occur in the general education classroom, it is essential that the structure of the class be able to support this approach. Otherwise, valuable learning time is lost, and students fall further behind as they miss out on core instruction. That's why the structured teaching framework discussed in chapter 2 (the gradual release of responsibility) is vital for RTI. A classroom that operates in whole-class mode from bell to bell is not one that is conducive to supplemental intervention. While overreliance on whole-class instruction is commonly thought to be a secondary-level problem, the statistics on this type of instructional practice at the elementary level are alarming. Pianta, Belsky, Houts, and Morrison (2007) studied the instructional climate of 2,500 elementary classrooms in first, third, and fifth grades. The researchers' findings were similar across the grade levels—students averaged over 91 percent of their instructional time in either whole-group instruction or individual seatwork. Only 7 percent of their time was ever spent in a group of five or fewer students. Class size alone cannot explain this, as the researchers reported that some classes they studied had only ten students enrolled. Given that student-teacher interactions are considered to be an indicator of effective teaching (see, for example, Bergin, 1999; Raphael, Pressley, & Mohan, 2008), it seems that many classroom teachers are not capitalizing on an element that contributes positively to interest, motivation, and learning.

A classroom structured around a more sophisticated design is one that has many opportunities for productive group work. When students are working collaboratively, it is an ideal time for the teacher to meet with a small group of students who are receiving Tier 2 supplemental instruction. Take Minh's classroom as an example. Ms. McLean has structured her classroom so that students meet daily in their literature circles to discuss the books they have selected. She uses some of this time to meet with small groups who need more instruction. Some of this work occurs as part of her core program. For instance, she participates in each literature circle weekly so that she can provide guided instruction. Additionally, she has the two RTI Tier 2 groups we have described. She provides them with supplemental intervention beyond the guided instruction she offers each group. She sees these students in both Tier

1 and Tier 2 groups, but in different configurations. "I actually don't do much whole-group instruction anymore, but we're getting more done," she says. "I've learned that getting up close with students increases their learning. Plus, it's hard to go to sleep when you're in a small group," she notes with a smile.

Without question, small-group instruction and intervention involve more than just pushing desks together. In the next section, we will describe the instructional moves that occur in small-group guided instruction and why these are so useful for students receiving supplemental supports.

Guided Instruction in Small Groups

Guided instruction is the time when the teacher instructs and scaffolds in order to extend the cognitive reach of the learner. Consider the purpose of a scaffold at a construction site. It is temporary, and it allows the worker to do something she couldn't do without it there. She can reach further, or lift more, because the scaffold is there (Greenfield, 1999). In the same way, teachers provide scaffolds to support and extend student learning.

The purpose of guided instruction differs in Tier 1 and Tier 2. During core instruction, the purpose is to explore the extent to which students are beginning to assume cognitive responsibility, or—as one of our colleagues puts it—"to see what stuck." For example, when Ms. McLean meets with literature circles in Tier 1, she is looking for evidence of the students' use of previously taught literary skills. In Tier 2, direct explanation and modeling take on a more dominant role. Lessons in Tier 2 typically begin with teacher-led instruction, followed by scaffolds. These lessons are designed to build background knowledge, refine procedural knowledge, and encourage meta-cognitive awareness. When Ms. McLean meets with a Tier 2 supplemental intervention group, she actively teaches information and then uses scaffolds to gradually release responsibility. In addition to her direct explanation and modeling, she uses questions to check for understanding, prompts to activate procedural knowledge, and cues to shift attention (Fisher & Frey, 2010).

Direct Explanation and Modeling

In direct explanation, the teacher provides a clear statement about what will be taught and how it will be used. In addition, the teacher uses a think–aloud process (Davey, 1987) that alerts the student to the decision making that accompanies the strategy or skill being taught. The statement of what is to be taught is closely related to establishing purpose, a teaching behavior shown to be particularly effective with English learners (Dong, 2004/2005; Hill & Flynn, 2006). Guided instruction in Tier 2 often begins with establishing purpose and thinking aloud through modeling, as the intent in supplemental intervention is to build knowledge and raise language levels.

Ms. McLean begins a lesson with Minh and the others by stating the purpose ("We're going to preview tomorrow's *Peter Pan* reading and look for examples of literacy devices we've been studying in class") and then providing direct explanation ("As I read, I am going to think aloud about what I'm noticing as I read. Please follow along with your eyes on your text while I read"). After she models noticing the role the swans play in the scene, disapproving of Peter's foolish ways, she says, "They remind me of the adults he's trying to avoid." Pausing for effect, she continues, "I think the author is using a large, beautiful, but haughty bird to symbolize how adults seem to Peter," she tells them.

Questioning to Check for Understanding

Guided instruction must necessarily include checking for understanding in order to devise one's next instructional moves. A well-crafted question allows the teacher to determine what students know and don't know at that moment. Depending on the response, they may need additional background knowledge, a review of a procedure or a process, or a clarification to clear up a misconception. After modeling how she thinks about the symbol of the swans, Ms. McLean asks, "What kind of a personality do you expect a swan to have?" Minh and the others give her a puzzled look, and Minh says, "How can bird be a hottie?" Ms. McLean pauses, then laughs when she realizes what has just occurred. She goes on to explain, "Here's what the word *haughty* looks like [she writes it on the chart paper]. I don't mean a *hottie* like you all say about a good-looking person [they giggle]. That word looks like this [she spells it under the first word, then crosses it out]." Ms. McLean defines *haughty* and quickly uses other synonyms so they will understand what she is referring to.

Questioning to check for understanding can also occur at the end of the lesson. This is a great time for collecting information for progress monitoring, such as completing a checklist or other instrument. At other times, questioning at the end of the lesson can be for the purpose of seeing what instruction "stuck." Ms. McLean ends many of her lessons with a peer summary. She instructs students to explain what they learned to a partner, and she listens to ascertain what has been retained. "It gives me an idea of what I need to do next," she says.

Prompting to Spur Cognitive and Metacognitive Thinking

Prompts serve as a type of scaffold that extends the student's ability to do something she might not otherwise be able to do alone. The intellectual space created by closely replicating a cognitive or metacognitive move with the guidance of a more competent other allows the learner to focus on what she is doing, how she is doing it, and why (Reiser, 2004). Prompts can be generally described in four dimensions:

- *Background knowledge prompts* focus on the cognitive aspect of a concept, skill, or strategy and invite the student to use what she already knows to solve a dilemma. When Ms. Ortiz says to Yazmin, "Use what you know about holidays to think of reasons why people celebrate Thanksgiving," she is prompting the child to use her background knowledge.

- *Procedural or process prompts* cause the learner to consider a step in a sequence of cognitive behaviors. When Eduardo's math teacher, Mr. Simon, reminds the student to "think about how you will set up the problem to find the function of *y*," he is using a procedural prompt.

- *Heuristic knowledge prompts* focus on the informal problem-solving approaches we use. Making a list of items before going shopping is a heuristic; so is filling up the gas tank of the car because you know you'll be putting on a lot of miles running errands. Heuristics are used in academic tasks, too. For example, a math student might draw a picture of the number of items in a word problem, and a biology student might highlight the definitions she's written in her notebook. When Ms. McLean reminds Minh to "make a list of pros and cons about Peter's life in Neverland," she is prompting her student to use a heuristic to resolve a question.

- *Reflective knowledge prompts* require the learner to notice his own learning. We use these frequently throughout guided instruction, asking questions like "Does that make sense to you?" or "Are there any other ways you could answer that question?" The purpose of a reflective prompt is to spur metacognition, often described as "thinking about thinking." Metacognition is closely associated with language learning, as awareness of one's learning is believed to make learning itself easier (Chamot, 2005). Consequently, an EL student who is cognizant of her use of cognates or who uses an English-Japanese dictionary to clarify her understanding of a difficult word is metacognitively aware. In these two cases, metacognition is also making the learning of some heuristics easier as well!

Prompts can be phrased as questions ("How will you know you're done?") or imperatives ("Try finding the corner pieces of the jigsaw puzzle first"). They may be speculative ("I wonder what would happen if you tried 'earthquakes in North America' in the search engine?") or even leading ("And the prince and the princess lived . . ."). The intent of prompts is to scaffold a learner's performance of a task so that he or she can complete as much of it on his own as possible. At times, prompts can involve "chaining" a task either forward or backward. *Forward chaining* refers to getting the student started on a process—for example, teaching the first line of a song, followed by the second, the third, and so on, until the student has learned the entire sequence. In *backward chaining,* the teacher sings the entire song, except for the last line, which the student completes. Soon the child is singing the last two lines, then the last three lines, and so on, until he or she is able to sing the entire song alone. In the same way, prompts may come as a series of scaffolds that assist the student in learning the steps in a complex process, such as making a prediction about a text or calculating the perimeter of a rectangle. Forward and backward chaining are especially useful for students who are very new to English and are learning simple conversation dialogue.

Cues

While prompts are intended to trigger cognitive or metacognitive thinking, they sometimes lack the specificity a learner may need at that moment. A cue is a physical, verbal, or visual signal that shifts the learner's attention to the source of the answer. As when a teacher asks questions to check for understanding, the response the student offers to the prompt lets the teacher know whether he or she needs to follow up with a cue. When a prompt fails to elicit a correct response, a cue, which is more overt, can direct the learner to the correct answer or necessary information. Teachers use a pattern of questions, prompts, and cues throughout their instruction but are not always conscious of the instructional moves they are making. Labeling these behaviors can be useful for mentoring novice teachers as they support English learners.

Cues come in several different forms and represent a loose continuum of scaffolds. The most overt are physical cues, such as placing one's hand over the child's to guide handwriting. Physical cues also come in the form of a guiding touch, such as a tap on the elbow to signal the direction of a movement. These cues can be faded to gestural cues, in which the teacher points but does not touch the student, as when pointing to a diagram on the page of the textbook. These can be faded still further to positional cues, in which an object is deliberately moved to focus the student's attention on it. For instance, Yazmin is using a laminated T-chart and word cards to sort verbs and adverbs. When she has difficulty, Ms. Ortiz slides the word card "walking" a few inches nearer to the verb column.

A verbal or visual cue to further strengthen effectiveness usually accompanies these physical, gestural, and positional cues. This technique is especially useful when teaching English learners, as the simultaneous presentation of physical, verbal, and visual cues increases the number of modalities through which the student can receive information. The pairing of cues to engage the verbal, auditory, and kinesthetic senses is a hallmark of instruction for students who are learning new concepts while also learning a new language (August & Shanahan, 2006). As Ms. Ortiz moves the word card to draw Yazmin's attention to it, she also says, "This card says, 'walking.' Is that an action?" The combination of a verbal cue (reading the card) and a prompt (a leading question) is enough scaffolding to enable Yazmin to place the card in the correct category. In addition, Ms. Ortiz has several visual cues at her disposal. The main one in this interaction is the T-chart Yazmin has in front of her. This visual cue allows Yazmin to keep herself conceptually organized as she completes the task. Ms. Ortiz also has a word wall in the classroom organized into parts of speech. Had Yazmin not been able to complete the task correctly with these cues, the teacher would have shifted the student's attention to the word wall to prompt the girl's background knowledge about verbs and adverbs. If this had still proven inadequate, Ms. Ortiz was prepared to use direct explanation and modeling to reteach.

In guided instruction, the number and types of instructional moves one makes can be overwhelming to catalog. Our goal is not to exert effort in sorting these out, but rather to describe a general framework of practices that foster a gradual release of responsibility. In Tier 2 intervention, this shifting of responsibility is typically accomplished by first offering direct explanation and modeling of the task, skill, or concept, followed by questioning to check for understanding. When a student fails to provide evidence of understanding, reteaching is in order. If the student does show reasonable understanding, then some of the cognitive load is shifted to her as she tries it on for herself. When she runs into difficulty, the teacher provides prompts to elicit cognitive or metacognitive thinking. If this is inadequate, the scaffolding is further strengthened with a combination of physical, verbal, and visual cues that shift the learner's attention to the sources of information she needs. The goal at all times is to provide the minimum amount of support needed in order for the student to do the cognitive work. This is at the heart of scaffolded learning and is an essential practice for continually transferring cognitive responsibility in a learning environment that encourages students to take risks.

Frontloading

Some students come to school already having been exposed to academic content and skills before they are taught. Consider the following examples of the experiences some students have had that can affect their understanding of the content being discussed in school:

- Micah and his family go to museums every Tuesday to take advantage of free admission. He's seen the planetarium show as well as the collections of the art museum, natural history museum, and science center.

- Brittany's family traveled to the Kennedy Space Center to watch the shuttle launch. In advance of the trip, they read extensively about the space travel program on the NASA website. Brittany was exposed to a lot of technical vocabulary related to the solar system and exploration of space.

- Alejandro attends a summer school camp, and has for several years. During the most recent program, the students studied animal adaptation, visited the zoo, and created murals about biodiversity.

These students will probably perform better in school, at least in specific units of study, because of the experiences they have had before formal learning takes place. In psychology, this concept is known as *priming*. Traditionally, priming is thought about in terms of the impact that one stimulus has on reactions to future stimuli. A classic example of this process involves showing people an incomplete sketch and slowly revealing more of it until they recognize the picture. Later, these people will identify the sketch at an earlier stage than was possible for them the first time (Kolb & Whishaw, 2003).

Malcolm Gladwell popularized the concept of priming in his book *Blink* (2005). As one example, Gladwell relates the study of two Dutch researchers who had two groups of students each answer forty-two *Trivial Pursuit* questions. One group was asked to take five minutes to think about what it would mean to be a professor and write it down, while the other group was asked to do the same with *soccer hooligan* in place of *professor*. The students who thought about professors ended up getting 55.6 percent of the questions correct, while the soccer group got 42.6 percent correct.

In education terms, we think of this method as *frontloading*. While the psychology experiments are often conducted in relatively short time spans, frontloading is done over hours or days. In general, frontloading involves strategically preteaching the background knowledge, vocabulary, and language structures students need to comprehend the lesson (Harper & De Jong, 2004). Of course, there are situations in which the entire class requires frontloading. For example, our chemistry and physics colleague Maria Grant recently frontloaded her students on the concept of stoichiometry (the quantitative relationship between reactants and products in a chemical reaction) because her assessment data suggested that they needed it. There are very few students who have experience with these kinds of tasks:

> How many moles of chlorine gas (Cl_2) would react with 5 moles of sodium (Na) according to the following chemical equation?
>
> $Na + Cl_2 \rightarrow NaCl$

While frontloading can occur in Tier 1, quality core instruction, it is more often conducted with small groups of students based on identified needs. As can be surmised from the student examples above, not all students need frontloading, and spending valuable instructional time providing this support for all students would not be wise. For our purposes here, it is important to remember that not all English learners will benefit from frontloading in a given lesson; teaching is based on what students already know and understand—not the fact that they're learning English. Having said that, English learners require frontloading more often than native speakers of English because of the language demands of school.

Background Knowledge

As noted in the experiences of the three students introduced in the opening of this section, background knowledge varies tremendously. Background knowledge is one of the best predictors of understanding. In other words, the more one knows about a topic, the more likely one is to understand additional information about that topic.

Unfortunately, teachers often assume that their students have the necessary background knowledge to access the curriculum. Too often, this is not the case, and students struggle with the task simply because they do not have a bank of experiences to draw on. Developing and activating background knowledge requires, first and foremost, that the teacher understand the prerequisite information that is assumed in a given lesson. We like to think of this in terms of *core* versus *incidental* background knowledge (Fisher & Frey, 2009a). As a quick example, a lesson comparing Cinderella stories around the world assumes an understanding of fables and fairy tales as core background knowledge. It would also be useful if students knew one version of the story with which they could compare others, so we might consider that to be core background knowledge as well. Incidental background knowledge might include concepts about princes and princesses, fairy godmothers, and formal evening events.

Background knowledge is a key consideration when planning instruction and intervention that is culturally responsive. As noted earlier, accounting for experiences, culture, language, and social roles is essential when planning lessons (Brown & Doolittle, 2008; Gay, 2000). There is a tendency to evaluate background knowledge in terms of deficits, thinking only of what the child may be missing. However, a culturally responsive lens regards background knowledge as an asset as well. What unique experiences, traditions, and knowledge does the child possess? This mindset is far more demanding, because the teacher may be less knowledgeable about something than the student.

For example, first-grade teacher Ms. Sanchez has planned a supplemental reading lesson for Seyo and another girl that uses a book in which the main character pours tea for a visitor. The teacher asks how the girls' families make people feel welcome. Seyo explains the coffee ceremony her mother performs when guests are in their home, while the other child, whose family comes from Chile, discusses the *mote con huesillo,* a cold, sweet drink made with peaches, that her family serves in the summer. Ms. Sanchez goes to the language chart the class is creating and adds these two examples of using beverages to make someone feel at home.

At other times, students may need to have some background knowledge built. The students who need the core background knowledge, whether they are English learners or not, most likely need small-group instruction that builds and activates that knowledge. This serves to prime (as in "prime the pump") learning for the rest of the lesson.

Consider a lesson on the Pilgrims and their experiences coming to North America. This content works well for students who grew up in the dominant culture in the United States. They've heard stories about Pilgrims and have probably had some sort of Thanksgiving celebration. Depending on their age and grade, they may already know about the native peoples of the Americas, the *Mayflower*, Plymouth Colony, Puritans, religious persecution, and reasons for immigration.

For Yazmin, our third-grade student receiving supplemental intervention, and her peers to be successful, they need relevant background knowledge to be built. While the other students are working in their groups, Ms. Ortiz meets with a small group of students to frontload their background knowledge related to Pilgrims. She starts with a book, *If You Sailed on the Mayflower in 1620* (McGovern, 1991), because in the absence of direct experiences, reading is one of the best ways to build background knowledge (Marzano, 2004). Of course, she doesn't have the students read the book by themselves, because she knows that they still need their background knowledge to be built. She also knows that the rest of the class doesn't need to hear her read this book, as they have the background knowledge and skill level to read it, if they so choose, as part of their independent reading selections.

As she reads the book aloud to this group of students, she pauses to talk about the contents with them. Sometimes she models her own thinking, and other times she invites the students to make connections based on their own experiences. For example, when she gets to the part about the problems the Pilgrims had in Plymouth, the group stops to talk about sickness. The text says, "By spring, about half of the Pilgrims and sailors were dead" (p. 49). The text continues, noting that the graves were not marked because the Pilgrims did not want the Indians to know how many of them had died. In their discussion, the students comment on the Pilgrim's experiences:

Marco: They died almost all. They no celebrate.

Yazmin: They was probably sad. My gramma died of sickness, and we was sad.

Omar: How is everything going on? How they life now?

Marco: Some is still alive. The other ones, they help sick ones.

Yazmin: They is scared of Indians, but the Indians would help them, right?

Marco: No, no help. They is enemies.

Omar: No, they help. They have dinnertime together.

As this excerpt of their conversation suggests, this group of students is wrestling with the ideas from the book and what they already know. Their teacher interacts with them to ensure that they have enough background knowledge to derive benefit from the Tier 1 instruction they will receive. Of course, these students also receive supplemental interventions related to language development, but spending time on background knowledge is an important part of their Tier 2 support.

Background knowledge can be built in other ways, not just by reading and discussing a text in class. Some teachers send reading materials home in advance so that students can talk about them with their siblings or other family members. Others use graphic organizers to help students organize background knowledge information, and still other teachers demonstrate processes or directly explain information for students.

For English learners, realia can also be used to build background knowledge. Realia, real objects related to the unit of study, range from insects to menus to clothing items—just about anything that will help the student understand the lesson. Smith (1997) suggests that we also use virtual realia, which he defines as "digitized objects and items from the target culture which are brought into the classroom as examples or aids and used to stimulate spoken or written language production." A world history teacher we know brings artifacts from her travels to use as realia in her class. In one lesson, she used trench art to facilitate a group of students' understanding of the conditions of World War I. Another colleague uses guppies to demonstrate how fish move through water, in order to facilitate observation of displacement. In each of these cases, the teacher is focused on building background knowledge so that the students will benefit from the core instruction.

Vocabulary

Teachers can also frontload vocabulary. Like background knowledge, vocabulary is a significant predictor of understanding. In other words, when one knows the words, one is more likely to understand the content. Vocabulary is one of the greatest instructional needs English learners have (see, for example, Watts-Taffe & Truscott, 2000; Webb, 2009). As we noted with background knowledge, however, not all students need to have vocabulary frontloaded for them. Frontloading specific vocabulary for students who need it assumes that content vocabulary will also be taught as part of the core instruction. Frontloading vocabulary should supplement, not supplant, core vocabulary instruction.

In terms of instructional design, frontloading vocabulary works a lot like frontloading background knowledge. The teacher first identifies which words are critical to understanding and then determines which students do not understand those words. Meeting with those students as part of a supplemental intervention provides the teacher with an opportunity to build the success of students in the core program.

Once in the group, the teacher has a lot of options for preteaching the selected words. As with core vocabulary instruction, frontloaded vocabulary instruction must be meaningful, and students require multiple exposures to really understand a word. A few of the more common approaches to frontloading vocabulary for English learners include the following:

- *Semantic maps*—These are visual displays of information that help students learn words and see their relationship to other words. Typically, the main concept is included in the center circle, and related ideas are placed in the smaller circles. These can continue out further and further as students explore targeted words. Figure 4.1 shows a semantic map that Eduardo created as part of his supplemental instruction in science. In addition to the concept words, relational words are added to the lines between the circles so that students also learn some of the terminology that aids in retelling information. This strategy is especially helpful for English learners, as they often confuse relational words, which hampers their academic development.

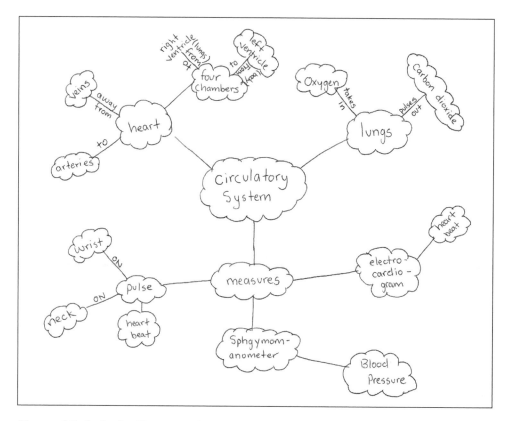

Figure 4.1: A student's semantic map.

- *Word cards*—When teachers want to focus students on specific words, they can use word cards. Based on the Frayer model (Frayer, Frederick, & Klausmeier, 1969), these cards are usually created from three-by-five-inch or five-by-seven-inch index cards, which are divided into four quadrants. The targeted word is written in the upper left-hand quadrant. The word's definition, written in the student's own words after the teacher explains the meaning, is included in the upper right-hand corner. What the word doesn't mean or a non-example of the word is written in the bottom right-hand corner. In the bottom left-hand corner, the student illustrates the meaning of the word. Figure 4.2 shows a sample word card from Eduardo's science class.

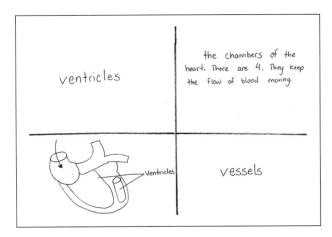

Figure 4.2: A science word card.

- *Total Physical Response (TPR)*—This is an approach in which movements are associated with specific words (Asher, 1966). It is most commonly used with students new to the language of instruction but can be used to focus students on concepts that are important to learn. TPR can be as simple as following motions with commands ("Take out your math book. Place it on the desk.") or as complicated as retelling a story such as *Five Little Monkeys Jumping on a Bed* (Christelow, 1998).

In addition to using these instructional routines, teachers sometimes provide students with a direct explanation of targeted vocabulary words. For example, Mr. Dexter, Minh's math teacher, knows that she and three other students who receive supplemental intervention do not know the meanings of the words *estimate* and *reasonableness,* as related to the math lesson they will be receiving. As part of his supplemental intervention, Mr. Dexter meets with this group of students and uses direct explanation and a series of examples to familiarize them with the concepts in advance of the lesson. Through trial and error, example and non-example, the students in this group acquire an acceptable understanding of the concepts behind these two words so that they can participate in the core instruction. While this isn't the sole focus of their supplemental intervention, the students in this group would fall further behind if Mr. Dexter did not provide this support for them.

Language Structures

In addition to building their background knowledge and vocabulary, English learners need to know that English is a language system that can be analyzed and used methodically (Slavin & Calderon, 2001). As Dutro (2007) points out, in order to frontload language, the teacher must analyze the language and cognitive demands of the lesson and ask him- or herself the question: What language is essential for students to be able to express their understanding?

Asking this question often leads to the conclusion that students must develop an understanding of grammar and syntax. Thus a common use of supplemental intervention time is teaching students the rules of English. As Dutro says, "Students need to learn English, not just *in* English." Which rules should be taught has been the subject of much debate (see, for example, Gascoigne, 2002). Most advice on this issue suggests that teachers should look at students' current proficiency levels compared with state standards and focus their grammar instruction accordingly (Berger, 2001). Most textbooks and reading programs provide a scope and sequence of grammar and syntax that can be used for supplemental intervention.

In addition to learning specific grammar rules, English learners benefit from the use of sentence and paragraph frames. These frames provide students with the support they need to develop academic literacy. College composition experts Gerald Graff and Cathy Birkenstein (2006) recommend the use of frames (they call them "templates") as an effective way to develop students' academic writing skills. They defend the use of frames or templates by noting:

> After all, even the most creative forms of expression depend on established patterns and structures. Most songwriters, for instance, rely on a time-honored verse-chorus-verse pattern, and few people would call Shakespeare uncreative because he didn't invent the sonnet or dramatic forms that he used to such dazzling effect. . . . Ultimately, then, creativity and originality lie not in the avoidance of established forms, but in the imaginative use of them. (pp. 10–11)

As is the case with several of the other instructional routines, sentence and paragraph frames can be used in both Tier 1 instruction and Tier 2 interventions. The difference is the content of the frames and the practice that students receive in using them. For example, over several supplemental intervention sessions, Eduardo was taught the following frames as part of his social studies class:

- I think _____ is important because _____.

- I agree/disagree with _____ because _____.

- I agree with _____ (source) that _____ (opinion/perspective) because _____.

- Both _____ and _____ are alike/different because _____.

- _____ happened because _____.

- This event in history reminds me of _____ because _____ (making connection).

- Due to the fact that _____ (cause), _____ (effect) happened.

These frames provide Eduardo an opportunity to use language and to internalize the grammar and syntax rules of English. In other words, they apprentice him into the world of academic English. Over time, and with the practice provided in supplemental intervention, Eduardo will begin to use these frames automatically and will vary them based on the situation and context he wants to talk or write about.

Language frames are not just for older students. Ms. Sanchez regularly uses them with Seyo and other students in her first-grade class. Many of the language frames she used at the beginning of the year focused on asking for and offering help to one another:

- Could you help me with _____, please?

- I think you should try _____ to see if it will work.

Other language frames are specific to the content, such as these introduced in reading:

- I can predict _____ because _____.

- I like this story because _____.

- This story reminded me of _____.

Although these frames are routinely used in other parts of the school day, Ms. Sanchez makes a point of using them during supplemental instruction with Seyo. She usually writes them in advance on chart paper or a small whiteboard and cues Seyo to use them in her discussion.

Feeding Forward

Classrooms are engaged in a number of formative assessment functions at any given time. We describe these as feeding up, feeding back, and feeding forward (Fisher & Frey, 2009b). Feeding up is the process of establishing purpose during initial instruction, a process more fully described in chapter 2. Feeding back—the mechanisms we use to respond to student work—can be verbal ("You made a great choice by beginning your speech with a rhetorical question. It got us interested right away.") or written, such as circling or underlining passages in an essay and writing comments in the margins. The third component in a formative assessment system is feeding forward, and it plays an important role in Tier 2 intervention.

Feeding forward is the process of making instructional decisions about what needs to be retaught. It is usually set into motion when the teacher has probed to check for understanding and the student has demonstrated that he or she does not yet understand what has been taught. In many cases, this failure to grasp a key concept becomes a barrier to future instruction. To be sure, the operative word in that last sentence is *key*—as much as we love our content, it is not imperative that students learn everything we teach. However, when something is critical, such as mastering the letters and sounds of the alphabet or factoring polynomials, we cannot simply hope for the best and figure that students will pick it up eventually. The knowledge and skills that are critical to acquire may include facts, concepts, processes or procedures, or familiarity with the conditions under which any of these are used. Some knowledge may be interesting, but not essential for mastery. In other words, as we have noted, there is a difference between incidental knowledge and core knowledge (Fisher & Frey, 2009a). This distinction is an important one for Tier 2 interventions, as this valuable instructional time needs to be devoted to the kind of knowledge that will result in advancement in the core curriculum.

It is helpful to have a decision-making model for determining whether something is core or incidental in nature. For supplemental interventions, we would argue that feed-forward instruction focus only on core knowledge. Determining whether or not something is core requires an analysis across four dimensions: representation, transmission, transferability, and endurance (see table 4.1).

Table 4.1: Decision-Making Model for Identifying Core and Incidental Knowledge

Core Knowledge		Incidental Knowledge
The information is foundational to understanding the main concepts	**Representation**	The information may be interesting but is peripheral to the main concepts
Requires multiple exposures and experiences	**Transmission**	Can be explained or defined easily (using a label, fact, or name)
Will be needed again to understand future concepts	**Transferability**	Specific to this concept; unlikely to be used in the future
Will be remembered after details are forgotten	**Endurance**	Details and specifics are not likely to be recalled later

Source: Fisher, D., & Frey, N. (2009a). Used with permission.

Representation refers to whether the information is representative of the main concept being taught. Core background knowledge is foundational to the concept, whereas incidental background knowledge is peripheral. By way of example, few would disagree that knowledge of alphabetic principles is foundational for a beginning reader; knowledge of the story *The Very Hungry Caterpillar* (Carle, 2008) is interesting but not foundational. A second question has to do with the way the information is *transmitted*. Some knowledge requires lots of repetition and exposure, while other information can be explained easily. The ability to compare and explain the relative size of two objects in first-grade math requires lots of opportunities and might well warrant additional instructional opportunities; naming the animals used in comparative statements ("Which one is bigger, an emu or a canary?") is incidental and is probably not core knowledge for this task. Ms. Sanchez makes decisions such as these as she plans Tier 2 intervention lessons for Seyo.

Some of the concepts and processes we teach are essential for future learning; in other words, they possess a high degree of *transferability*. Memorizing multiplication facts is worth the time and effort because the fluent retrieval of this information is critical in performing more complex mathematical procedures in later years. In contrast, copying a multiplication table from the board has little transfer and is not worth devoting time to during a Tier 2 intervention lesson. The final dimension to be analyzed in determining core knowledge is whether the information has an *enduring* quality, meaning that the essence will be remembered long after the details have been forgotten (Wiggins & McTighe, 2005). An understanding of Shakespeare's importance as a figure of Western literature is enduring; the details of iambic pentameter are not.

Deciding what constitutes core knowledge versus what is incidental is not easy or straightforward. In fact, some of these decisions are likely to be a source of disagreement among educators. However, we believe that these conversations are part of the healthy debate that is critical to a professional learning communities process. Given that Tier 2 intervention time is so valuable, it is essential that it not be used to deliver more Tier 1 instruction. Small-group guided instruction is a part of good Tier 1 instruction; Tier 2 intervention must focus on the core knowledge that serves as a gateway to making progress in the overall curriculum.

A feed-forward system in RTI requires both frontloading and, at times, reteaching of information that has been previously presented to students. We don't subscribe to the "say it louder and slower" reteaching method we have unfortunately witnessed, as it is unlikely that what didn't stick the first time is going to do so the second. Instead, Tier 2 intervention that involves reteaching should adhere to the following set of principles to ensure quality:

- *Vary the task so that it is not a duplication of what has already been taught.* Teachers should consider other pathways or examples that might reinforce the concepts, procedures, or processes they are teaching. This increases the likelihood that students will make a connection to previously learned material.

- *Make the reteaching interesting by using games, manipulatives, and high-interest activities.* The beauty of a small group is that teachers can accomplish a lot more in a shorter amount of time. Teachers should make sure that they are keeping the pacing quick as they use high-interest activities. These activities can be motivating as well and help to offset the boredom than can creep in.

- *Prepare questions in advance to check for understanding.* Teachers should think about how they will check for understanding during the lesson. We often prepare key questions in advance and write them on a sticky note so we remember to ask them. Questioning is a vital part of a guided instructional lesson, and one that can be overlooked in the rush to teach rather than guide.

- *Have a variety of prompts and cues at the ready.* Teachers should consider the teaching devices present in the environment, such as the poster listing the steps of the scientific method or the magnetic letters on the whiteboard. As well, they should think about the kinds of prompts they can offer when the learner gets stuck, and they should have them on hand so they can use them in a timely way.

- *Increase repetitions to ensure that the practice effect occurs.* A major purpose of reteaching is to give the student more opportunities to practice using the concept, skill, or strategy. Teachers should make sure that the lesson is not filled with lots of direct explanation and little practice. Students need the chance to practice under the teacher's tutelage.

- *Provide guidance to ensure that students practice correctly.* Having said that, a Tier 2 intervention lesson can't be devoid of anything other than practice. Students need guidance in practicing correctly. We have a colleague who points out that "practice doesn't make perfect; practice makes permanent." Scaffolded instruction must shape student learning so that it is continually improving in accuracy, fluency, and competence.

- *Make peer-to-peer reteaching part of the lesson.* One way to increase the number of repetitions and build competence is to have students in the group teach one another. This allows the teacher time to witness growing understanding and to provide further guidance as needed. In addition, it gives students a little more cognitive responsibility in taking on the role of the teacher. Teachers can also do a role reversal and have students teach them what they have learned.

SOLUTIONS FOR TEACHING ENGLISH LEARNERS

1. Utilize a professional learning communities structure to facilitate conversation among educators. The response to intervention process requires teacher collaboration, and the PLC is an ideal structure for teachers to work together. At Tier 2, a number of decisions need to be made: What students will participate? For what purposes? The various educators on a staff possess knowledge about instruction and learning theory, as well as information pertaining to individual students. While the classroom teacher has a pivotal role in Tier 2 intervention, specialists such as the reading coach, bilingual or language development specialist, and special educator can offer insight into methods for designing and implementing intervention lessons. Additionally, grade-level or department colleagues are able to make decisions about core knowledge and identify successful approaches for teaching it.

2. Make sure that supplemental intervention does not replace core instruction. Although stated before, it bears repeating: students who receive Tier 2 supplemental interventions also need—in fact deserve—access to quality core instruction. If students miss core instruction, they're at risk for falling further behind. If supplemental instruction is designed to correct poor core instruction, teachers burn out because of the overwhelming numbers of students who need help. Said another way, thirty or so minutes of supplemental intervention can't compensate for six hours of poor instruction. Importantly, not all English learners need supplemental intervention. Students who are not making progress in quality core instruction do need extra guided instruction. It's unequal resources for unequal needs; that's fair.

3. Guided instruction must be intentional, must be based on student needs, and must result in student understanding. Supplemental intervention is not a conversation between students and their teacher. It's a time to focus on specific students who are not making progress. To be intentional, the teacher must identify the core knowledge or skill required by the task and directly teach that through a combination of direct explanations and modeling, questions to check for understanding, prompts to facilitate cognitive and metacognitive work, and cues to focus students' attention. The outcome of each of these sessions should be increased student understanding; none of us have time to waste!

4. Supplemental instruction includes frontloading and feed-forward instruction. Beyond core instruction, English learners who are not making progress need to have background knowledge, vocabulary, and language structures pretaught to them. This ensures that they get the most possible from core instruction and provides them with an opportunity to make more rapid progress. In addition, English learners who are not making progress need feed-forward instruction that is based on their performance. These reteaching events must focus on core concepts and push students to higher levels of understanding and performance.

CHAPTER 5

Tier 3: Intensive Interventions and Decisions About Learning Language Versus Learning Disability

WHEN WE LEFT EDUARDO, he was making progress. It seemed that the supplemental interventions were taking hold and that his performance was improving to the point that he might not need interventions at all. But midyear, that changed. Eduardo stopped making progress, and the teachers at his grade level noticed it within a week, thanks to their progress monitoring.

During their team meeting, Eduardo's English teacher, Ms. Jacobs, is emphatic. "I don't believe in plateaus," she says. "Students just don't do that. There has to be something getting in the way of Eduardo's learning. Let's review his data graphs and see what we can do to get him back on track."

As is her habit, Ms. Sawyer, the reading specialist, is quick to display student achievement charts on the interactive whiteboard. As the group of teachers begin their review process, Ms. Sawyer says, "Let's just pause a minute and remember where he came from. Look back at the screening data we had from August; he's grown a lot. Yes, there's still a ways to go, but we've had a very positive impact on him."

Nodding in agreement, Ms. Armento, the bilingual special educator, adds, "Yes, he really is one of our success stories. His spelling has improved, and his oral comprehension, according to the SOLOM, is much better. I wonder what's going on with him and what we should do about it."

Mr. Jimenez, the physical education teacher, notes, "It's great for me. He's now telling a whole group of students what we'll be doing each day and how different sports are played. He really has much better comprehension. Even his vocabulary is improving."

After a relatively long pause in which the teachers are looking at one another and at the data charts, Ms. Jacobs continues. "That's the risk we face, right? To back off when students are successful. He's worked really hard and has developed great relationships with all of us, and his peers. But he's still really far behind, and I'm worried that he may slow down again and end up back where he started. We have to accelerate his achievement; that's what we agreed to do. We don't settle for good, we go for great. And his writing isn't great."

Ms. Sawyer, nodding in agreement, responds, "You're right. He can do more, and we're the team that can help him get there. It's time to step it up a notch. I think he's a prime candidate for intensive intervention. He responds to the interventions we provide, so let's see what we can do with him one-to-one. And I agree with you that writing is a great place to start."

Ms. Armento, holding a few of Eduardo's writing samples with their attached analyses, says, "I think that he's taking more risks and writing more, especially with longer sentences and more complex ideas. This means that the errors are starting to show up and we're seeing more of them. But I agree that he really needs intensive intervention if he's going to gain control of his writing. I'd like to take this on. I think that he and I can work together to address these grammar errors. We've got to get those corrected soon, or he'll leave us and go to high school as a struggling writer."

Ms. Sawyer adds, "And the rest of us can keep up the good work on core instruction and the supplemental things we're already doing. They're working, and we don't want to stop those. He needs six-plus hours a day of great experiences and the added thirty minutes of intensive intervention could be the breakthrough he needs. [Pauses as the teachers nod in agreement.] Okay, who's next? Any other students who aren't making progress in their supplemental interventions?"

Ms. Jacobs, getting teary-eyed, says, "Thank you all. I just can't thank you enough. In all my years of teaching, I couldn't have ever imagined that we could come together and focus on the learning of specific students. I really love my job!"

Defining Tier 3, Intensive Interventions

While Tier 2, supplemental intervention for English learners, was fairly easy to define, Tier 3 has been harder to understand and implement. As Echevarria and Hasbrouck (2009) explain:

> In some RTI frameworks, Tier 3 includes special education services for students who have been formally identified as having a learning disability and have had an Individualized Education Plan developed for them. In other cases, schools design Tier 3 to be an intensive, focused intervention that may include students without disabilities. In some cases, Tier 3 is supplemental—provided in addition to Tier 1 and Tier 2 services. In other cases, particularly when the student's performance level is far below grade-level expectations, Tier 3 may be provided as a replacement to core classroom instruction. (pp. 2–3)

In our experience with English learners, Tier 3 intensive interventions are different from special education services. Tier 3 is another level of support—another attempt to ensure that students receive the best possible chance to succeed without being referred for special education services. When English learners do not respond to Tier 3 intensive intervention, then special education services may be considered. Remember, unlike the "wait to fail" days, in which it could take several years before supplemental supports were provided, in RTI, students who experience difficulty and are not making progress receive added instruction (intervention) right away.

For our purposes, we set an expectation that Tier 3 intensive interventions require individualized instruction that lasts at least thirty minutes per day for at least three (but hopefully four or five) days per week. While others note that Tier 3 has been conducted with small groups of students (see, for example, What Works Clearinghouse, 2009), when schools can provide individualized intensive interventions, students benefit (Barton & Stepanek, 2009; Fuchs & Fuchs, 2009). While the mindset in Tier 2 is "more," the mantra in Tier 3 is "most" (Illinois ASPIRE, 2009), as in:

- The most **time** (core program + supplemental intervention + intensive intervention)
- The most **intensity and frequency**
- The most **scaffolded instruction**
- The most **expert teachers** providing instruction
- The most **language support**, especially vocabulary
- The most **opportunities for students to receive feedback**
- The most intensive **motivational strategies**
- The most frequent **progress monitoring**

In their review of Tier 3 intensive interventions for English learners, Vaughn and Ortiz (n.d.) provide the following guidelines for implementation:

- ELLs who are significantly behind in reading require highly intensive and extensive reading interventions that start immediately (as early as 1st grade) and continue until the student is able to adequately benefit from reading instruction provided within the core classroom instruction.

- Tier 3 intervention needs to be provided by a well-trained specialist such as a bilingual education or an ESL teacher with a strong background in literacy, or a learning disability teacher who has a strong background with and understanding of the educational needs of ELLs.

- Tier 3 instruction may need to last for a significant period of time when students are making minimal progress; adjustments to instruction may need to be made, with consideration given to the integration of contextual factors (e.g., family, personal, and classroom variables) that may need to be addressed as necessary. A team approach to problem solving may be very useful in interpreting factors that influence progress and providing suggestions for designing instruction.

- Students who have been provided research-based reading interventions that are typically associated with improved outcomes may not demonstrate significant gains and may require highly individualized reading instruction that considers other factors such as attention, language and vocabulary development, and behavior problems. A team approach to problem solving that considers many of these factors may facilitate the development of an appropriate instructional plan. (n.p.)

In sum, for English learners, Tier 3 ideally involves individual instruction that addresses the needs identified through screening tools and other assessments. This level of intervention is reserved for students who have not made progress in Tier 2 supplemental interventions or who are so far below grade level when they enter a US school that they are seriously at risk for not catching up to their peers or even for dropping out of school altogether. Tier 3 requires that the following components of the student's learning experience be intensified:

- Time
- Expertise
- Assessment
- Family involvement

Time

Time refers to the length and frequency of the individualized instructional sessions as well as the overall duration of the intervention itself. As previously noted, the sessions are typically thirty minutes in length but can be as long as sixty minutes. An important consideration in determining the length of the session is the stamina of the student. In one-to-one teaching, the task demand is high, and younger students, as well as those with less language proficiency, are going to find these sessions to be especially taxing. We would rather have thirty productive minutes with an on-task student than sixty minutes marked by fatigue and flagging effort.

A general recommendation for the overall duration of the intervention is that it last a semester or so (about eighteen to twenty weeks). The point is to ensure that the student has received adequate instruction of a sufficient duration to presume gains. Duration of intervention, as with session length, is dependent on the learner and the purpose. Therefore, the expected length of the intervention should take into account the expected development of the needed skills, in particular keeping in mind that second language development is a complex process.

In some cases, duration may be cyclical. Our work with elementary school English learners has focused on "academic booster shots" that are offered over the first years of school (Frey, Lapp, & Fisher, 2009). A longitudinal study of eighty-five English learners who received eight weeks of daily, thirty-minute intensive instruction in first, second, and third grades found that this approach resulted in a steady closure of the achievement gap in reading. Before the first intensive intervention, these students averaged 65 percent lower on measures of reading achievement than their peers who were not identified for the intervention. By the end of the third eight-week session two years later, the group averaged 17 percent lower than their peers who had never participated in the intervention. While they remained lower in third grade than those who had never needed intervention, their achievement level marked a stark contrast to where they were in first grade and represented a trajectory noticeably different from the one usually expected, in which the gap becomes wider each year (see, for example, Chall & Jacobs, 2003). In addition, because these one-to-one intensive intervention sessions lasted for eight weeks in each school year and were repeated each school year, we were able to minimize lost Tier 1 core instruction. (A later section of this chapter will address the logistics of coordinating individualized interventions with core instruction.) Although a booster shot approach is not recommended in every case, it is worth considering, especially with young English learners who may need periodic intensive intervention at the beginning of their school careers.

The frequency of sessions is another variable in designing an intensive intervention. Daily sessions hold the advantages of making scheduling easier and offering distributed practice. However, daily sessions may not be feasible or necessary. In designing intensive interventions, a good rule of thumb is to schedule the intervention in proximity to the opportunities to use the skill in the classroom. For example, a middle school student on a rotating block schedule might have English only four days a week. In this case, it might be more effective to schedule sessions on those four days in order to keep the student in alignment with his English course and to give him opportunities to use in class what he is learning in his intensive intervention sessions.

Expertise

Another variable that is intensified in Tier 3 intervention is student access to expertise. While reading coaches, bilingual specialists, special educators, and related services personnel such as the speech/language pathologist are consultative in Tier 1 and used intermittently in Tier 2, they take on a more direct role in Tier 3. In some cases, they assume primary responsibility for designing the intervention, collecting assessment information, and providing instruction. How a school chooses to deploy its resources will vary, but in Tier 3 all resources should be considered. The collective wisdom and individual specializations available can mean the difference for some students. Keep in mind that the goal of RTI in general, and of Tier 3 in particular, is to eliminate the possibility that a lack of access to quality instruction might explain persistent underachievement. We recognize that involvement in Tier 3 interventions is balanced against the other responsibilities that these specialists have. But placing resources on the table is the only fair thing to do, and administrators must also be considered. In our high school, Doug and Nancy have primarily teacher leadership roles but also possess reading and language expertise that should not be overlooked. Therefore, they each work individually with a small number of students each year who need Tier 3 one-to-one intensive interventions. When each credentialed adult assumes responsibility for some Tier 3 students, the overall workload is lightened. In addition, this approach embodies the maxims of most mission statements that advocate "doing whatever it takes" to increase achievement.

Assessment

A third factor that is intensified in Tier 3 intervention is assessment. As in Tier 2 supplemental intervention, progress monitoring should be frequent, even weekly or daily. This close progress monitoring allows the teacher to detect whether the student is responding positively, and whether the focus of instruction needs to change. Tilly (2002) advises reexamining existing assessment data and collecting new information before moving into Tier 3 intensive interventions. This would entail taking another look at Tier 1 screening data, examining the trajectory of performance on curriculum-based measures in Tier 2, and reviewing records and classroom observations. In particular, it is useful to collect information using an ecological inventory perspective, meaning an analysis of the specific environments, to determine where and when difficulties arise, and where and when they do not (Tilly, 2002).

In addition to frequent progress monitoring, assessment in Tier 3 takes on more of a diagnostic aspect. While many diagnostic assessments exist (and are beyond the scope of this book to discuss in great detail), it should be noted that the same experts mentioned in the previous section also have specialized training in administering specific diagnostic assessments for the purposes of refining instruction. For example, the reading specialist may use the Rapid Automatized Naming and Rapid Alternating Stimulus Test (RAN/RAS) if problems with processing speed are suspected (Wolf & Denckla, 2005). A speech/language pathologist might use the Test of Oral Language Development—Primary (Hammill & Newcomer, 2005) to examine aspects of sentence imitation, relational vocabulary, and articulation. Special educators and bilingual/language development specialists also have a battery of assessments at their disposal. The use of assessments in Tier 3 is a sensitive issue and is not meant to circumvent the regulations in IDEA 2004 regarding referral and testing for special education. Rather, we are focusing on the collection and analysis of assessment data specifically for improving instruction. As always, families are important partners in the RTI process in general, and with regard to assessment in particular.

Family Involvement

We have reserved a detailed discussion of family involvement for this chapter, but in fact it is essential in Tiers 1 and 2 as well. As many have noted, the family is the child's first teacher and is the keeper of a child's educational and personal history. The family should not be an afterthought ("Oh, yeah, don't forget to call the parent"), but rather should be an integral part of the child's team. This can be especially important for the families of English learners, who are often themselves learners of a second or subsequent language. In addition, these students' families may possess a different perspective of schooling, given their own experiences and cultural expectations.

It is vital that involvement for families of English learners be sensitively crafted to acknowledge their norms of communication and engagement. In order for home-school partnerships to be improved, schools must take it upon themselves to become more "homelike," rather than always expect homes to become more school-like (Frey, 2010). The qualities of home include affection and appreciation, commitment, positive communication, the ability to cope with a crisis, and time together (Stinnett & DeFrain, 1985). The need for trusting relationships is especially great in Tier 3 intensive interventions, where families become a vital source of information, support, and advice.

Table 5.1 (page 108) lists the indicators for high levels of family involvement (Johnson, Mellard, Fuchs, & McKnight, 2006) and shows how they can be customized for families of English learners. In addition to being recipients of the everyday communications regarding the logistics of field trips and school lunches, families must be able to see themselves as valued partners and know that they are considered critical to solving problems as well.

Individualized Instruction Is Necessary for Intensive Intervention

There is a fair amount of evidence that individualized, 1:1 instruction improves achievement. For example, a meta-analysis of thirty-one studies of 1:1 reading tutoring programs found that "well-designed, reliably implemented, 1:1 interventions can make significant contributions to improved reading outcomes for many students whose poor reading skills place them at risk for academic failure" (Elbaum, Vaughn, Hughes, & Moody, 2000, p. 617). In their study of students' response to intervention in mathematics, Ardoin, Witt, Connell, and Koenig (2005) found that four of the five students identified as most at risk made significant progress with individualized instruction as part of Tier 3 interventions.

Table 5.1: Improving Family Involvement for English Learners

Family Involvement Standard	Refined Standard for Families of English Learners
Parental notification includes a description of the problem; clear, unambiguous documentation that shows the specific difficulties the child is experiencing; a written description of the specific intervention and who is delivering instruction; a clearly stated intervention goal; and a long-range timeline for the plan and its implementation.	Notification is in both written and verbal form and delivered in the home language.
Parents and staff reach mutual agreement on the implementation, plan, and timeline.	Families are asked for their perspectives before the plan is finalized, using their preferred modes of communication. In addition, the meeting place may be set for an off-campus location that is comfortable and convenient for the family.
Parents frequently receive progress data.	Progress data are furnished in the home language and include information for interpreting and understanding the results.
Parents are actively supported to participate at school and at home.	Schools become more "homelike" in order to capitalize on the child's strengths.
Parent questionnaires and surveys assure parents that the school values their opinions.	Opinions may be solicited through other modes, including oral surveys administered by a trusted parent educator.
Parent questionnaires and surveys assure school staff that parents find school staff and school programs (e.g., interventions and instruction) to be of high quality.	Information is presented to the school staff by parent educators and family representatives in order to provide a richer understanding of the data.
Parents view the implementation of due process procedures and protections as timely, adequate, and fair.	These processes are conducted in the home language and include a parent educator as intermediary for asking questions, providing information, and challenging perspectives.
School staff members strive to help parents feel welcome, important, and comfortable in the school setting.	The settings of both school and home are valued and are appreciated for their own strengths.

Source of family involvement standards (left column): Johnson, E., Mellard, D. F., Fuchs, D. & McKnight, M. A. (2006), p. 3.40. Used with permission.

We use six questions to guide our decisions as we develop a lesson for individualized instruction (Frey, 2006):

1 *What is the purpose of the lesson?* In planning intensive intervention for an individual student, the person providing this instruction has to clearly understand the purpose of the lesson. In addition, the purpose has to be communicated clearly to the student. In our experience with intensive interventions for English learners, the purpose has to be reviewed several times during the session because many of the students receiving this level of intervention cannot yet focus on the main point as they work to comprehend the language, and they may instead become distracted with related information or interesting bits of trivia. As we have noted previously, the purpose is focused on specific components, or skills, that the student has not yet mastered. In addition, the purpose must be linked with the skills needed to catch up to core instruction. One of the problems schools and teachers often encounter in implementing Tier 3 interventions is the pressure a new curriculum places on students. When the Tier 3 interventions are not linked with the core instruction and supplemental interventions, the student is at risk for falling behind in multiple areas. When this happens, valuable time is spent trying to catch the student up on the Tier 3 curriculum—time that could have been spent focused on access to the core curriculum.

2 *What are the student's background knowledge and prior experiences?* As we noted in chapter 4, background knowledge is critical to student understanding. In the lessons we profiled as part of Tier 2 interventions, teachers took background knowledge into account, and they must do the same when planning intensive interventions. In our experiences with intensive interventions with English learners, background knowledge has been a part of every lesson. Whenever we've neglected to include developing and activating background knowledge as part of an intensive intervention, the result has been less than satisfactory. In some individualized intervention lessons, background knowledge takes center stage and is the main purpose of the lesson. But this is rare. The amount of time spent on background knowledge in most lessons is incidental to the skill development that students need. It is important to remember, however, that EL students bring different sets of background knowledge to their studies. We need to be aware of their experiences in order to find ways to activate this knowledge, and we need to be aware of any missing pieces that may be critical to comprehension.

3 *What are the targeted skills or strategies for this lesson?* Selecting the correct skill or strategy is critical, and it is the hardest part of planning Tier 3 intensive interventions. As we noted in the discussion about purpose, the targeted skill or strategy has to be based on the learning needs of the specific student as well as the state standards for the student's grade level so that the intensive intervention provides the student greater access to the core curriculum. In our experience with English learners, the areas that are often targeted for building skills include:

- *Oral language development*—Reading and writing are related to speaking and listening. While the relationship between these input and output systems is complex (Butler & Hakuta, 2009), English learners have to develop all four systems to be considered proficient and to function well in English-speaking contexts. Our experience with English learners suggests that spending intensive intervention time on oral language with students who are most at risk builds their competence and confidence so that future intervention progresses quickly.

- *Phonemic awareness and phonics*— There are often sounds and corresponding symbols in English that speakers of other languages do not commonly use (see, for example, Brice & Brice, 2009). Our experience with English learners suggests that attention to this area falls into two extremes. Either phonemic awareness and phonics are utterly ignored or they are the exclusive focus of the intensive interventions. Neither approach is responsive to the needs of the learner.

- *Pronunciation*—English learners often make mistakes that interfere with their ability to communicate. Importantly, omissions, substitutions, distortions, and additions in pronunciation are part of a normal development pattern and should be the focus of intervention only when an individual student's progress lags significantly behind that of English-learning peers (Piper, 2006). Our experience with English learners suggests that the use of digital recorders, with which students can listen to their pronunciation and compare it with that of other speakers, can be motivating and highly effective in addressing this need.

- *Grammar and syntax*—The structure of the English language is difficult for many students (Larson, 1996) and can be the source of significant frustration and confusion for English learners (Ellis, 2006). Grammar instruction can be engaging and meaningful and can result in fairly rapid progress when it is aligned with identified needs. Our experience with English learners suggests that teachers can provoke errors by constructing tasks for the purpose of assessing grammar, and then they can immediately respond to the errors students make.

- *Figurative language* such as proverbs and idioms—These expressions confuse learners and permeate the texts students are expected to read. Nippold (2009) notes that figurative language is pervasive and can be used in at least four ways: to comment, as in "Blood is thicker than water"; to interpret, as in "His bark is worse than his bite"; to advise, as in "Don't count your chickens before they hatch"; or to warn, as in "It is better to be safe than sorry." Figurative language is beautiful but can be very hard to teach, as the ideas these expressions portray do not necessarily have the same meaning in other cultures. Our experience with English learners suggests that this area requires a great deal of attention.

- *Comprehension*—Making meaning is important in every subject and is affected by language proficiency. While there is evidence that components of effective instruction for native English speakers are effective for English learners (August & Shanahan, 2006; Goldenberg, 2008), there is also evidence that all English learners will not benefit from simply participating in core instruction (O'Day, 2009). Some English learners need explicit instruction in comprehension strategies that takes into account their proficiency levels, their prior experiences, and their cultural background (Manyak & Bauer, 2008). Our experience with English learners confirms Garcia's (1991) finding that many EL students comprehend more than they are able to communicate orally in English. In other words, not being able to tell their teacher what they think doesn't mean that students failed to comprehend.

- *Writing*—Communicating in this mode is important for both school and life beyond school. As we noted in the chapter on Tier 2 interventions, writing interventions must be based on the skills required to produce quality work rather than on common traits of good writers. When students participate in writing interventions designed around both form and content, they make considerable progress (Lee, Mahotiere, Salinas, Penfield, & Maerten-Rivera, 2009). Our experience with teaching English learners suggests that writing instruction improves reading achievement as well as writing achievement.

4 *How will essential vocabulary be taught?* As Wallace (2007) notes, vocabulary is among the most important skills English learners need to develop. When they have background knowledge, and the words for that knowledge, learning can focus on language structure and understanding. Direct instruction in vocabulary, combined with word-learning strategies, will most likely increase English learners' proficiency (Wallace, 2007). Our experience with English learners suggests that intensive interventions can focus on cognates, the meaning of basic words, and the multiple meanings of specialized vocabulary (Lapp, Fisher, & Jacobson, 2008).

5 *What will the student write or produce?* Students should create something as part of every intensive intervention lesson—not just those that focus

on writing instruction. The product could be a short written summary or something that requires a bit more time. Ending each session with a product ensures closure for the student and provides the person conducting the intervention with information about the student's understanding. In addition, the product can be used as an informal communication tool, alerting the student's classroom teacher to the focus of the day's intervention session. Of course, the product has to align with the purpose and the instruction to be effective. For example, when Eduardo's teacher focused on verb tense in one of the intensive intervention sessions, Eduardo used a series of sentence frames to produce examples, both in speaking and in writing, of his use of different tenses. In a session focused on retelling content information, Eduardo was asked to summarize the information in writing. In a session focused on comprehension, Eduardo drew a picture to convey his understanding and then wrote sentence explanations of each aspect of the illustration.

6 *What future skills will the student need?* As we have previously noted, intensive interventions should be linked with quality core instruction and Tier 2 supplemental interventions. They should also be linked with one another. To ensure that they are, the teacher must carefully examine the student's performance after each session. In essence, progress monitoring becomes a daily phenomenon. Of course, the data the teacher collects may vary each day, based on the focus of the lesson, but each lesson should be designed to reinforce previous learning and address identified need.

Scheduling Intensive Intervention

Much of the discussion in this chapter has focused on the importance of, and best practices for, one-to-one instruction. We imagine that this is causing some stress to readers who are thinking, "When can I do this? There's no time!" To be sure, providing individual instruction can be challenging. It is important to acknowledge that intensive intervention is likely to result in a tradeoff with core curriculum. That's why Tier 1 instruction must be tight. When a school has a common vocabulary for what constitutes sound instructional design, the conversation about what the student may be able to miss becomes more accurate. For example, the time when the teacher is establishing purpose for the lesson or modeling thinking is not time the student can afford to miss. On the other hand, a student's participation in productive group work could be replaced by an individual intervention session. The coordination of a responsive intensive intervention plan is only as good as the schoolwide planning that goes into crafting a responsive Tier 1 approach.

As with placing all the human resources on the table, so it goes with the school's temporal resources. Access to individual instruction can occur during the school day, especially when a "push-in" model is used. We are cautious about using pullout models, primarily because those arrangements can limit who is eligible to serve as an interventionist. Tier 3 intensive instruction is reserved for students who are not receiving special education supports and services. These students are protected from placement in special education without due process. A special educator is a valuable member of the RTI team and a potential interventionist, but it is advisable to make sure that if a special educator provides Tier 3 instruction, it is done within the general education classroom, where he or she is already delivering support to other students who have individualized education plans (IEPs).

In addition to delivering Tier 3 intensive interventions during the school day, schools should consider scheduling them before and after school. These extensions of the school day can be valuable opportunities for providing individual instruction, as long as they can be coordinated with family schedules and transportation can be arranged. Using before-, during-, and after-school times increases the number of students who can be served in Tier 3 interventions and ensures that students also access core instruction.

The intensive nature of Tier 3 interventions can tax the resources of the school, and although this level of support is effective for many students, there remain some for whom well-designed interventions do not result in improvement. Students who have not responded to intervention should be considered for possible special education referral. The fact that limited language proficiency can either mask or mirror a learning disability makes identification a complex issue. In the next section, we will examine this issue in greater detail.

Language Learner or Learning Disability?

Some of the errors that EL students often make can look very similar to those made by students with a language processing disorder, a language learning disability, or some of the most common learning disabilities, including those related to visual processing and auditory processing. These similarities sometimes make it difficult to distinguish between disability and the natural process of developing language proficiency (Kuder, 2007). Table 5.2 (page 114) presents some behaviors that are exhibited by both students with a learning disability and students who are learning English and identifies the possible causes of the behaviors for each group.

"How do we know if it's lack of proficiency in English or a learning disability?" This is the big question that has plagued educators since we first recognized the category of learning disability and then witnessed the large influx of English learners in our schools. Determining the answer is further complicated by the student's language and literacy proficiency in the first language, as those who are literate in one are likely to acquire a second language more easily, whereas those whose schooling has been interrupted may experience

Table 5.2: Language-Related Behaviors and Possible Causes

Evidence/Behavior	Learning Disability	Language Learning
Confuses similarly shaped letters (for example, b/d, p/q, m/n)	Visual acuity Visual discrimination Working and long-term memory	Unfamiliarity with the Roman alphabet Lack of prior schooling Lack of experience with written text
Does not consistently recognize words or letters	Visual acuity, processing or object recognition Working and long-term memory	Overload of new vocabulary and learning
Forgets previous learning	Auditory or visual processing Lack of transfer and generalization Working and long-term memory	Cognitive overload Lack of background knowledge Lack of oral language skills or vocabulary knowledge
Poor handwriting	Visual acuity Fine motor control Visual-motor integration	Unfamiliarity with the Roman alphabet Lack of prior schooling Lack of experience with written text
Disorganized writing	Language planning Executive function Working memory and retrieval	Unfamiliarity with Western patterns of organization Vocabulary
Unable to sound out words or rhyme words	Auditory discrimination Hearing loss Phonological memory Working memory	Lack of knowledge of English sounds of letters and blends
Retells a story out of sequence or in a disorganized manner	Sequential processing Pragmatic language Executive function Working and long-term memory	Did not understand the language of the story Forgets story details or sequence while focusing on comprehending individual words and phrases Inexperience with Western literature
Does not follow directions	Auditory processing or memory Hearing loss Behavior	Does not recognize the role of "signal" or "transition" words

difficulties in learning English (Collier, 1987). In addition, the nature of the first language can exert its own influence on the acquisition of English. As an example, Case and Taylor (2005) describe English as an "opaque language," meaning that the sound/letter relationship is a weak one (p. 130). Students who speak and read Spanish, with its strong letter/sound relationships, may have initial trouble with decoding the letter/sound relationships in English.

Case and Taylor (2005) have identified three categories in which there is overlap between the language development of English learners and that of students with disabilities:

- Pronunciation: Omissions, substitutions, and additions.
- Syntax: Negation, word order, and mood.
- Semantics: Forms of figurative language such as proverbs, metaphors, and similes. (p. 128)

Fortunately, an RTI model that emphasizes instruction, rather than measurement, helps with making the decision to refer an English learner for special education testing. When we analyze the student's response to instruction and, subsequently, to intervention, we tease out the important effects of language proficiency, or lack thereof, on performance without letting the distinction between language learning and learning disability paralyze us into inaction.

Readers will recall that Yazmin and Eduardo received supplemental and intensive interventions and made progress. In contrast, Minh and Seyo are still experiencing difficulties with school. Let's look at the next steps in their educational journeys.

A Profile of Minh

Soon after Minh arrived at her new high school, she participated in the screening done with every student, including the Gates-MacGinitie Reading Test (MacGinitie, MacGinitie, Maria, Dreyer, & Hughes, 2000) and a math assessment. Because Minh was a designated English learner, Ms. Prejean, the bilingual specialist, reviewed her state language assessment from eighth grade and personally administered a new one. "I was surprised when I saw how low her score was last year, and I compared it to the number of years she had been in English-speaking schools," Ms. Prejean said later. "I wanted to check on her use of language myself." The results showed that Minh had not advanced since a year earlier. "That's when I did some other language assessments, and then inputted the information into the STELLA [Selection Taxonomy for English Language Learner Accommodations] online decision-making website to review possible testing and instructional accommodations for her," she said. (STELLA was developed by WIDA and is available at no cost to educators. To view the STELLA generator, visit http://elladvantage.com.)

Fortunately, Minh's school has a sophisticated RTI system in place, so her teachers were notified, and Ms. Prejean followed up with each of them a few weeks later to see how Minh was progressing in Tier 1 core curriculum and instruction. Even with the accommodations in place, Minh was having difficulty keeping up. Minh began participating in Tier 2 supplemental intervention in the first nine-week term, receiving support in oral and written language in class from Ms. McLean, who consulted with her special education and ESL colleagues in her professional learning community.

Curriculum-based measures of Minh's writing were collected and analyzed, but after twelve weeks had changed little. When the end of the second term arrived, the RTI team acted quickly. Minh began attending Tier 3 intensive instruction, now getting individual writing support from Ms. Prejean. Despite this, Minh's writing showed little improvement, as evidenced by a writing sample Ms. Prejean collected in May of Minh's ninth-grade year. The sample was a response to the prompt *Compare life in your home country to life in the United States.* As shown with earlier student samples, Ms. Prejean marked the word sequences with carets as correct or incorrect and underscored incomplete sentences.

^Hi^! ^My^name^is^Minh^. ^I^was^born^in^Ho^Chi^Minh^City^. ^Vietnam^is∨beautiful^country∨have∨beaches^, rivers^, mountains^, and∨hills^. ^I^lived^in^Vietnam^from^the^day^I∨birth∨to^see^the^ beautiful^country∨arrive∨my∨7^years^old∨birthday^. ^My^family^ and^I∨leave^my^homeland^and^beautiful^country∨has∨traditional∨ generation^and∨generation∨came^to^United∨State∨with^the^ papers∨reunite∨of∨ domestic∨. ^Thanks∨my^uncle^helped^my^ family^do^the∨papersa∨and^bring^together ^my^family∨∨come∨ to^United∨State∨. ^When^I∨was∨lived^in^Vietnam^, I∨have^hard ^working∨to∨study^in^my^school∨of∨each^period^because^Vietnam^ is^a^country∨has ∨good^education^and^culture∨traditional∨ generation∨and∨generation^.

An analysis of Minh's writing shows the following:

1 Total words written (TWW): 119
2 Average number of words written per minute (AWPM): 2.6
3 Total words spelled correctly (TWSC): 115
4 Total number of complete sentences (TCS): 5/8
5 Average length of complete sentences (ALCS): 11.2
6 Correct punctuation marks (CPM): 12/13
7 Correct word sequences (CWS): 93
8 Incorrect word sequences (ICWS): 38
9 CWS – ICWS = 55

In Minh's writing, we see many errors in both syntax ("Thanks my uncle") and word choice ("from the day I birth"). However, the ratio of errors to correct word sequences is high (about 1:3), as is the number of fragmented sentences. Minh also has a very low written fluency rate (less than three words per minute over a forty-five-minute time period), and, most importantly, she did almost no comparing at all, despite the focus of the writing assignment.

The RTI team met with Minh's parents to determine what should be done next. Through an interpreter, Minh's father said that while his daughter always reassured the family that all was well at school, he could see the many late nights she spent doing homework. The team agreed that Minh worked very hard in her classes, but effort and instruction weren't getting her far enough along. With the family's support, the team referred her for special education testing, and over the summer Minh met with the school psychologist and the special education teacher to complete a number of assessments, including one in Vietnamese, one in English, and several non-language-based assessments. The assessment in Vietnamese identified the same areas of difficulty in her primary language as in English, an important factor in distinguishing the difference between learning disability and the normal course of language acquisition. Minh was found to have visual processing and visual integration difficulties, and thus she qualified as having a language disorder and a specific learning disability. In September of her tenth-grade year, the team met to analyze the results of both her responsiveness to interventions and the language testing. "We decided to do both," Ms. Prejean said. "We weren't sure if we were missing something."

A Profile of Seyo

Seyo's arrival in the United States as a three-year-old predated any opportunities to acquire written literacies in her first language, so the only formal instruction she had received was in English. She and her family spoke Tigrinya in the home, but Seyo was rarely exposed to written forms of that language. After spending nearly a year in the Head Start preschool in her neighborhood, Seyo entered kindergarten, where the benchmark assessments her school used showed slow but steady progress through May.

The following September, Seyo entered first grade. Her teacher, Ms. Sanchez, used DIBELS as a screening tool during the first week of class. She compared Seyo's results to her scores from the previous year and saw that the child had lost ground. For instance, her phoneme segmentation score at the end of kindergarten was 9, already considered to be at risk. In early September of first grade, this score had declined to 7. Other subtests showed similar decline, so Ms. Sanchez carefully monitored Seyo's progress for the next few weeks, using simple maze assessments to see if the resumption of classroom instruction would improve her skills. By October, Seyo had not improved, and so she participated in eighteen weeks of Tier 2 supplemental instruction.

Because Ms. Sanchez did not know much about Seyo's background and culture, she turned to the school's speech/language pathologist and the family involvement coordinator for further information. Ms. Sanchez was surprised to learn that because the written form of Tigrinya dates to the early nineteenth century, there are not many written works. In addition, she learned that many Eritrean families speak and write in several languages. With the help of the school's parent involvement center, Ms. Sanchez contacted Seyo's family and was invited for a visit to their home. She learned that the family used Arabic for more formal purposes, including academics, while reserving Tigrinya for social language. Seyo's mother, she discovered, had been a teacher herself in Eritrea, and had taught her children the *abjad,* the Arabic writing system.

Ms. Sanchez's visits to Seyo's home established a positive relationship with the girl's family, and the discovery that both women were teachers gave them common ground for conversations. At school, Ms. Sanchez met regularly with Seyo and four other students who were having difficulty with beginning reading acquisition, including sound/symbol relationships, comprehension, and retelling. Knowing that Seyo had been exposed to Arabic, she speculated that the girl's difficulty with directionality of print in English might be due to her experiences with a writing system that is read from right to left. Whenever Seyo started on the wrong side of the page, Ms. Sanchez would cue her by pointing to the left side of the page.

Although some of the students showed gains during this period, the guided reading and writing lessons did not result in much in the way of improved achievement for Seyo. By mid-February, she was reading at a level 4, far below other English learners in the class. In addition, Ms. Sanchez was beginning to notice that Seyo's comprehension was lagging and that she appeared to have difficulty retaining details of the story and retelling them in an organized way. In fact, most of her retellings, even of familiar stories, were disjointed, rambling, and difficult to follow.

Before embarking on a more intensive Tier 3 reading intervention, Ms. Sanchez met with the speech/language pathologist. The teacher learned from the speech/language pathologist that the traditional tales from Seyo's home culture might be different from those in her books at school. The specialist explained that a story-grammar approach to analyzing a retelling (character, plot elements, sequence, and so on) might be inadequate. She suggested using a dynamic assessment approach of test-teach-retest (Gutierrez-Clellen & Peña, 2001). Dynamic assessment is believed to be an effective way of teasing out differences between language disorders and language acquisition problems, which, as we have noted, can often appear similar (Peña et al., 2006). Ms. Sanchez learned that normally progressing English learners will score higher on the retest, while EL students with language disorders show little gain.

The speech/language pathologist modeled a Tier 3 intensive reading lesson for Ms. Sanchez and introduced Seyo to some fundamentals of effective story-telling, including establishing the setting and time, introducing characters, and using dialogue. Ms. Sanchez began her lessons by reading Seyo a short story and then having the girl retell it, which served as a pretest. She then taught about story elements, including settings, characters, and events, and then read a similar story together with Seyo. After they read the story, the student retold it, using the book to support her. At other times, Ms. Sanchez told Seyo a story with no visual supports, and again the student retold it. These were particularly taxing exercises, and the dynamic assessments Ms. Sanchez collected on these occasions resulted in even lower scores.

Ms. Sanchez continued to meet with Seyo's mother to fill her in on her daughter's progress, and by mid-April both women were in agreement that while Seyo's effort was strong, she was not making the kind of progress they had hoped for. Seyo was referred for special education testing, which revealed a pervasive auditory processing disorder that negatively affected her ability to discriminate phonemes in words; follow spoken directions; and retell, summarize, and explain extended information.

While Seyo qualified for special education on the basis of a specific learning disability and a language impairment, this identification did not result in a magical change. However, when she went to second grade, both the speech/language pathologist and the special educator were regularly a part of her classroom. Her new teacher, Mr. Hall, was grateful for the information and support. "I feel like I'm already 'hitting the ground running' with Seyo," he remarked at the beginning of the year. By the middle of her second-grade year, although she was still struggling with reading, Seyo had progressed to a level 16. "She's on her way," Mr. Hall said.

What is Special Education?

Before we go any further, we have to make one point clear. We think of special education as a service, not a place. Accordingly, students with disabilities should receive ongoing access to core instruction, supplemental and intensive intervention, and an array of supports and services, as outlined in their IEPs, within their regular classrooms. With a few exceptions—such as articulation therapy or large-muscle movements as part of physical therapy—the majority of supports and services can and should be provided to students with disabilities within the regular education classroom. Minh doesn't suddenly drop off the radar of the school now that she has qualified for special education supports and services. Now, however, a different system of resources is mobilized to support her in her classes.

Minh remains on track to earn a high school diploma. Therefore, it is essential that she have access to the general education curriculum so that she can meet course competencies. In addition, Minh lives in a state that has a high-stakes graduation test. While she will receive accommodations on the test, she still needs to know and understand the content. Because the state exam has a writing component, improving her writing skills is imperative. Minh's special education teacher (called an "advocate teacher" in her school) meets regularly with the general educators to determine what learning approaches work best. Mr. Carruthers, Minh's tenth-grade biology teacher, discovered that Minh did quite well taking notes using an interactive note-taking system and then writing summaries using it as a guide. Minh's advocate teacher soon had a similar system for Minh to use in all her classes, and she steadily improved throughout the year.

That process is at the heart of inclusive education. As do all students, those with IEPs benefit from the collective wisdom of educators who pay attention to their successes. A primary role of special educators is to transmit successes between teachers and from year to year (Castagnera, Fisher, Rodifer, Sax, & Frey, 2003). Both Minh's and Seyo's schools use a tool for doing exactly this. Figure 5.1 shows the student profile that Minh's special education teacher completed for her English teacher.

This document is used to summarize useful information about a student with an IEP. This does not replace the requirement for all teachers to read the IEP.

Student name: Minh   **Grade:** 10   **Age:** 16   **Date:**

Special education teacher: Dietrich   **Technicians:** Tyson (Math/Science), Riviera (Eng/History)

General education teachers: Carruthers, Winters, Majerski, Donalds

---

IEP skills addressed in this class

1. Make inferences and draw conclusions after listening or reading narrative or expository text.

2. Answer cause-and-effect questions after listening to or reading a literary or expository text.

3. Write an expository composition about a specific topic that contains events in sequence, details, transitions, and a closing summary.

Areas of strength/interest

Minh is a friendly and positive person. She enjoys working with small children. Minh is able to share her thoughts, feelings, and questions with trusted adults. She has been in ballet folkloric for the past 10 years.

Minh likes to read books about "real people." One of her favorite books is *The Outsiders* by S.E. Hinton. Minh hopes to go to school to prepare to work with young children, perhaps as a preschool teacher. She speaks Vietnamese and works in her family's business.

Successful learning strategies/modifications/accommodations needed

Minh does well in small groups; she works well with her peers. In whole-group settings, she tends to be very quiet and is not always comfortable talking in big groups. She needs clarifications when given directions but is not likely to seek this help. She does best when information is given in an auditory form, with visual supports. She has had success with using an interactive note system to organize her writing. She is an English learner and struggles with the grammatical demands of the language. This shows up in her writing. It is helpful to encourage her to have a peer read her writing aloud to her so she can hear it and make corrections.

Communication strategies

Minh is extremely shy, and it takes some time for her to participate verbally in class. She is self-conscious about her oral language ability in English and will often sit quietly. She feels most comfortable in small groups and one-on-one. She is very well mannered, and when she feels comfortable with trusted adults, she will communicate her thoughts and questions.

Positive behavioral support strategies

Minh is a very well-behaved student. She gets along well with her family, peers, and teachers.

Grading and assessment accommodations

Minh qualifies for extra time and having directions clarified on standardized tests. She qualifies for a grading accommodation on her quarterly grades, which will be entered by Ms. Dietrich.

Important family/health information

Minh has a very supportive family. Both parents are very involved in her education. They have limited English skills, so it is helpful to work with Ms. Nguyen to translate written messages and phone calls.

Figure 5.1: Minh's student profile.

When general educators continue to be directly involved in a student's education, their presence each year at the IEP meeting is more meaningful. Finally, another compelling reason for inclusive practices is the distribution of expertise among the professional staff. Special educators, especially those at the secondary level, rarely possess the content expertise to teach the kinds of courses students like Minh need to take to be successful academically. Few special educators also hold a teaching credential in physics, geometry, or English. General educators are credentialed based on their deep knowledge of the subject matter, and students with IEPs need access to this level of expertise. In the same regard, special educators have significant training in designing and implementing curricular, instructional, personal, and technological supports (Fisher & Frey, 2004). This is evidenced by the central role of the speech/language pathologist both before and after Seyo qualified for special education services. Her insights into Seyo's cultural experiences and methods for assessment ensured that the RTI process was meaningful. When Seyo did qualify, this specialist already knew Seyo and could offer her and her second-grade teacher a smooth transition.

Underrepresentation or Overrepresentation of English Learners in Special Education

We often hear concerned educators lament that EL students are overrepresented in special education. The reality is somewhat more complex, however. While overrepresentation may be the norm in some districts, a closer look at the data reveals that EL students may, in fact, be *under*represented in special education in other districts. According to the *Biennial Report to Congress* from the National Clearinghouse for English Language Acquisition (Office of English Language Acquisition, 2008), approximately 10.3 percent of students in US schools were classified as English learners. At the same time, EL students represented only 5.4 percent of the special education population (Office of English Language Acquisition, 2008). Juxtaposing these two figures reveals a discrepancy, leading one to wonder why there are fewer English learners receiving special education services than would be expected. If these figures are accurate, why do well-informed educators believe that ELs are *over*represented in special education?

In actuality, it would not be surprising to find a slightly higher percentage of EL students in special education than fluent or English-only students. Many EL students arrive in North America after years of living in refugee camps or other situations in which a lack of prenatal care, adequate nutrition, and medical services is common. All these conditions can contribute to a learning disability. We also see schools in which language development specialists are unable to distinguish between difficulties in learning English and difficulties in learning. As we noted previously, the distinction between language learning and learning disability is multifaceted and complex.

Another circumstance that contributes to overrepresentation is when the multidisciplinary team charged with determining eligibility does not include a staff member trained in EL issues. Students may have been placed in special education because of poor performance and a lack of progress rather than because of an identified learning disability.

In other districts, however, the situation is reversed. There are English learners in some schools who might benefit from special education services but are not found to be eligible for them because of a lack of bilingual assessors, a lack of appropriate assessments, or difficulty interpreting the assessments. We have even seen instances in which a student was not referred for assessment because appropriate services were not available. We have also been told that a student was not eligible for special education services because a staff member assumed, "The student is an English learner and simply needs more time to learn English and catch up." This was the case with Minh, who had been overlooked for years because she continued to sound like an early language learner. In addition, as a quiet and well-behaved student, she didn't draw the attention of her teachers. In some cases, the outdated practice persists (whether stemming from actual policy or assumed policy) of prohibiting special education referrals of EL students who have been in the country for less than two years.

In remedying these challenges, the new IDEA allows determination of eligibility to be based on the teaching and learning process rather than on discrepancy alone. While Minh's and Seyo's schools elected to gather other testing data, they did not need to rely solely on a significant gap between expected and actual achievement. Instead, each school's PLC team had nearly a year's worth of very good RTI data to examine, and augmented this with other diagnostic tests that shed further light on their respective students' strengths and weaknesses. This is exactly the kind of flexibility these newer provisions are intended to provide to families and educators.

Supports and Services for Identified Students With Disabilities

One of the questions teachers and parents often ask of school systems with sophisticated RTI models is "What else will you do if the student qualifies for special education services?" This is a very appropriate question, given that the student has had access to quality core instruction and a host of interventions designed to improve achievement and close the performance gap. When a student does qualify for special education, a number of additional systems of support are activated. These special education systems do not, however, replace the student's language development services. We'll review several of the additional systems and provide references for readers interested in additional information.

Formalization

One of the things that happen when a student qualifies for special education services is that the system becomes more formalized. The supplemental and intensive interventions outlined in an RTI plan are not mandatory, and thus teachers may or may not implement the plans that are developed. When supports are part of an IEP, however, students and families have legal recourse if those plans are not implemented. In addition, the IEP formalizes the role of several additional professionals. While Tier 2 and Tier 3 interventions might be provided by a special educator as part of an allowable incidental benefit, the special educator becomes key in the overall coordination of service delivery for students who qualify for special education services. In addition, when a student receives special education services, there are formalized dates and timelines for assessments, plan development, monitoring, and such. For more information about the special education service delivery system, see *The Fundamentals of Special Education: A Practical Guide for Every Teacher*, by Robert Algozzine and James Ysseldyke (2006).

Funding

While this is a sensitive subject, in most states, students with disabilities generate supplemental funds for schools and districts. This money may not be used to supplant other funds but may be used to enhance the education of students with disabilities and help offset the cost of providing them with a free and appropriate public education, as outlined in federal law. While each state has a different funding formula, in every state money flows to schools and districts to support students' educational needs. One of the ongoing debates between special education directors and their general education counterparts is the issue of encroachment, in which funds from general education are required to provide services for students with disabilities (see, for example, Parrish, 2001). Another debate centers on the amount of money the federal government should contribute to special education costs, given the federal role in educating students with disabilities (see, for example, Minow, 2001). Originally, the US Congress committed to contributing 40 percent of the funding for states' special education services under IDEA. The federal government historically has provided only 8 percent of the funding, although that has increased in the recent past and in some years has been nearly 15 percent. Regardless of these debates, when a student qualifies for special education services, some of the costs of providing those services are funded through state and federal mechanisms. For up-to-date information about funding-related issues in special education, visit the Center for Special Education Finance at http://csef.air.org.

Goals

The IEP that is developed for a student with a disability includes specific goals. These goals establish expectations for progress, indicate who is responsible for seeing that they are met, and provide a timeline for collecting and reporting data. In other words, the goals in an IEP formalize part of the system that was in place during Tier 2 and 3 interventions, but with much more accountability for the process. Annual goals have three parts: (1) direction of behavior (for example, increase, decrease, maintain); (2) area of need (for example, reading, social skills, transition, communication); and (3) level of attainment (for example, to age level, without assistance). A goal for Minh might be to "increase her writing fluency from 2.6 words per minute to 5 words per minute as measured by the teacher at the end of twelve months." Similarly, a goal for Seyo might be "to increase her ability to retell stories written at her instructional level." For more information on developing goals for students with disabilities, see *Writing Measurable IEP Goals and Objectives*, by Barbara Bateman and Cynthia Herr (2006).

Curriculum Accommodations and Modifications

When a student has a disability, he or she is entitled to specific accommodations and modifications as outlined in the IEP. *Accommodations* are changes to the access a student has to the existing curriculum, whereas *modifications* are changes to the curriculum itself. For example, common accommodations include large-print versions, the use of calculators, audio books, Braille versions, and so on. Modifications include fewer test items, reducing an assignment from four parts to two parts, rewording questions, providing visual aids, and so on. The IEP team—including the student him- or herself, the family, general educators, special educators, related services staff, and administrators—identifies specific accommodations and modifications. These are written into the plan and are to be used by all of the teachers who interact with the student. Documenting accommodations and modifications is important and is especially helpful when the student moves to a new school. These records allow the new school to hit the ground running with what has been successful for the student. In many states, colleges will accept information from a student's IEP for accommodations to college-level classes. While the federal special education law does not apply to colleges and universities, Section 504 of the Rehabilitation Act, which provides for support that students might need to be successful in higher education, does (US Department of Education, Office for Civil Rights, 2007). For more information about curriculum accommodations and modifications, see *Modifying Schoolwork,* by Rachel Janney and Martha Snell (2004).

Testing

The IEP team can also designate accommodations and modifications for the tests students are expected to take. These accommodations and modifications can be used on classroom tests or state-level accountability tests. The key to testing accommodations is familiarity. Students need to use the testing accommodations regularly to be able to use them effectively on state accountability measures. Common testing accommodations include:

- Presentation (e.g., repeat directions, read aloud, use of larger bubbles on answer sheets)

- Response (e.g., mark answers in book, use reference aids, point, use of computer)
- Timing/Scheduling (e.g., extended time, frequent breaks)
- Setting (e.g., study carrel, special lighting, separate room) (Cortiella, 2005, p. 1)

Unfortunately, in some states, when students use modifications, their performance is not valued in the same way as it would be if they did not use them. For example, in California, if a student uses a modification on the state accountability test, that student is automatically scored "far below basic," regardless of how well he or she does using the supports that were identified as part of the IEP. For current information about testing accommodations and modifications, visit the National Center on Educational Outcomes at www .cehd.umn.edu/nceo/default.html.

Figure 5.2 is a checklist of possible accommodations and modifications in curriculum, testing, and other areas.

Classroom Accommodations	
☐ Seat student near front of classroom	☐ Stand near student when giving directions or teaching
☐ Seat student near a positive role model	
☐ Additional accommodations:	
Instructional Support	
☐ Assign a study partner	☐ Allow student to audio-record lessons
☐ Pair students to check work	☐ Have student review key points orally
☐ Provide modified and/or supplementary materials	☐ Assign a study partner
☐ Allow use of audio, visual, or computer equipment	☐ Provide tutoring by _____
☐ Additional accommodations:	
Lesson Presentation	
☐ Write key points on board	☐ Provide visual aids

☐ Make sure directions are under-stood/simplify directions	☐ Provide a written outline of lesson
☐ Include a variety of activities dur-ing each lesson	☐ Use graphic organizers
☐ Break long presentations into shorter segments	☐ Teach through multisensory modes
☐ Additional accommodations:	

Assignments	
☐ Allow extra time to complete	☐ Reduce homework assignments
☐ Allow student to audio-record assignment/homework	☐ Simplify complex directions
☐ Shorten assignments; break into smaller segments	☐ Use self-monitoring devices
☐ Reduce the reading level of the assignment	☐ Provide structured routines in writ-ten words
☐ Require fewer correct responses to achieve grade	☐ Allow for dictated responses to longer assignments
☐ Provide study skills training/learn-ing strategies	☐ Develop reward system for home-work completion
☐ Additional accommodations:	

Test Taking	
☐ Allow open book exams	☐ Give exams orally
☐ Allow extra time for exam	☐ Read test items to student
☐ Allow student to give test answers on audio recorder	☐ Give take-home tests
☐ Reduce length of exam	☐ Use more objective items (fewer essays)
☐ Additional accommodations:	

Figure 5.2: Possible accommodations and modifications for students with disabilities. Continued →

Organization	
☐ Provide peer assistance with organization	☐ Assign a homework buddy
☐ Allow student an extra set of books for home	☐ Plan for frequent communication with parent
☐ Additional accommodations:	

Behavior	
☐ Praise specific behaviors	☐ Use self-monitoring strategies
☐ Allow for short breaks between assignments	☐ Keep classroom rules clear and simple
☐ Consistently provide consequences	☐ Provide extra privileges and rewards
☐ Cue student to stay on task (nonverbal)	☐ Allow nondisruptive movement
☐ Mark student's correct answers, not mistakes	☐ Increase immediacy of rewards
☐ Implement a behavior system	☐ Ignore inappropriate behavior that is not drastically outside of classroom limits
☐ Implement a time-out procedure	
☐ Additional accommodations:	

Integrated Support Services	
☐ Provide peer support • Assistance • Listening • Tutoring • Buddy system	☐ Provide school counseling
	☐ Provide adult mentorship
	☐ Refer to community agency treatment support groups
	☐ Refer to parent/family support groups
	☐ Provide instruction to assist with disabling condition
☐ Additional accommodations:	

Nursing Considerations	
☐ Provide rest periods	☐ Provide wheelchair accommodations
☐ Address dietary concerns	☐ Provide instruction re: disabling condition

Assistive Technology

For some students, specialized technology expands access to the core curriculum. While there are obvious types of technology, such as wheelchairs and TTY (teletypewriter) communication devices, some are less obvious. Consider the various ways that computers can be modified to increase usage by students with disabilities (see table 5.3). Through the IEP process, students with disabilities can access a wide range of assistive technology devices, and these devices can often be paid for with targeted funding. For more information about assistive technology, see *Connecting to Learn: Educational and Assistive Technology for People With Disabilities,* by Marcia Scherer (2003), or visit the Assistive Technology Center at www.assistivetechnologycenter.org or the Alliance for Technology Access at www.ataccess.org.

Table 5.3: Technology Accommodations for Computer Systems

Input Routes	Processing	Output Routes
Alternate keyboards	Abbreviation/expansion and macro programs	Braille displays and embossers
Onscreen keyboards	Menu management programs	Monitor additions
Interface devices	Reading comprehension programs	Screen enlargement programs
Joysticks	Writing composition programs	Screen readers
Keyboard modifications	Writing enhancement tools (such as grammar checkers)	Speech synthesizers
Keyboard additions	Light signaler alerts	Talking and large-print word processors
Sip-and-puff systems		
Optical pointing devices		
Pointing and typing aids		
Scanners and optical character recognition		
Trackballs		
Touch screens		
Voice recognition		

Related Services

Students with disabilities can access a range of professionals who provide related services, such as speech and language specialists, reading specialists, occupational therapists, physical therapists, counselors, orientation and mobility specialists, and behavior specialists. While some of these experts are probably working with specific students as part of their overall support of RTI efforts, their time is specifically allocated to qualifying students with identified needs. These specialists can provide consultative services for classroom teachers as well as direct services to students (see, for example, Prelock, 2000). For more information about the ways in which related services professionals support students with disabilities, see *The Beyond Access Model: Promoting Membership, Participation, and Learning for Students With Disabilities in the General Education Classroom,* by Cheryl Jorgensen, Michael McSheehan, and Rae Sonnenmeier (2010), and *Collaborative Teams for Students with Severe Disabilities: Integrating Therapy and Educational Services,* by Beverly Rainforth and Jennifer York-Barr (1997).

SOLUTIONS FOR TEACHING ENGLISH LEARNERS

1. Some students require intensive interventions to be successful. These interventions must intensify the learning experience for students in terms of time, expertise, assessment, and family involvement. They have to be individualized and occur regularly, for at least thirty minutes three times per week but hopefully more often.

2. The individualized, intensive interventions that English learners need have a purpose, have a clearly defined skill focus, develop background and vocabulary knowledge, result in student products, and are linked with both Tier 1 and Tier 2 interventions, as well as with future Tier 3 interventions. These intensive interventions can sometimes be delivered by classroom teachers, especially before or after school, but are more often delivered by other specialists within the school, such as Title I teachers, reading specialists, special educators, or speech and language specialists. In some schools, every credentialed adult—including the library/media specialist and the principal—provides some intensive interventions. Regardless of who provides the intensive intervention, it must be focused on student need, and progress must be monitored carefully.

3. Some students will not respond adequately to intensive interventions and may require special education services. Using the data collected as part of an RTI initiative, teams may recommend a specific student for further assessment to determine if he or she qualifies for special education services. These diagnostic assessments have to be considerate of the student's language and culture if they are to be valid measures. While determining the difference between learning language and learning disability has been difficult, some students require identification to access additional supports and services guaranteed in federal and state law.

CHAPTER 6

Commitment to RTI: A Framework for Success

THE SUCCESS OF ANY response to intervention model rests on two key factors: accurate assessments and effective instruction and intervention. Of course, clear definitions of these terms, and staff members who understand these definitions in the same way, are integral to success as well. In this book, we have defined effective instruction for EL students and offered a model of instruction that encompasses Tier 1 core curriculum, Tier 2 supplemental instruction, and Tier 3 intensive intervention. We have proposed a process for assessment that can be used to determine the student's response to instruction and intervention and to inform instructional planning. Finally, we have discussed the ways a special education system dovetails with other supports in the school.

The common vocabulary that comes from a focused, schoolwide RTI system has benefits that extend beyond English learners. Our work with elementary, middle, and high schools that have implemented this model has demonstrated to us that supporting students with diverse learning needs is possible. It does, however, require that the school be committed to identifying and meeting those needs—that it be "responsive to intervention." While most schools have mission statements declaring this commitment, practical concerns get in the way of full implementation.

Effective models of instruction rely on a philosophical framework—a set of mutually held assumptions, values, and practices. It is this framework that guides instructional assessment, planning, implementation, and reflection—that is, the teaching cycle. It also guides policy, organization, and professional development at the site and district levels. Let's examine the assumptions, values, and practices upon which the RTI model is based. If these assumptions are not held in common within a school or district, this is an excellent place to begin the professional learning community work. Of course, individual teachers can use our RTI model in their classrooms, but taking this to the site or district level requires conversations with peers and a shared understanding of assumptions, values, and practices.

Assumptions

Our model is predicated on specific assumptions. These assumptions are so fundamental to good teaching that we sometimes don't include them as we reflect on and discuss our practice, "assuming" that all our colleagues hold these beliefs equally. But the truth is that we have all entered the field of education with a variety of biases stemming from our prior knowledge and experience, that time and new experiences alter perceptions, and that the reality of a changing society, coupled with ever-increasing responsibilities for all of us, can push these underlying assumptions to the background. Effective implementation of RTI depends on teachers' holding these three assumptions:

1 All students can learn when we teach (not just tell).

2 All students can be motivated to learn.

3 All teachers are teachers of language.

All students can learn when we teach (not just tell). This is a simple enough concept, but one that strikes at the heart of beliefs about children and learning. Undoubtedly, we all believe that all children can learn. The question is, to what level do we believe they can learn? We've heard statements like these from well-meaning teachers who love their students: "Some students just aren't good at learning language." "They can't learn to do algebra until they know their multiplication facts." In place of focusing on what the student cannot do, teachers can look first for evidence of what the student can do and what is inhibiting progress. Then they can look for ways to build on the student's strengths and work around the obstacles.

The other part of this statement speaks to our role in learning. Teachers who brag about the high rate of failure among their students, incorrectly using this data point as evidence of the rigor of their classes, bewilder us. We regard a high failure rate as a failure in teaching. That may cause some to squirm uncomfortably, but as a profession we need to move beyond the mindset that presumes that all students learn in exactly the same way and at the same time. Our job is to educate, and that means that we need to exhibit a high level of persistence that collectively results in a system that doesn't give up on students when they don't learn something the first time. As well, we need to use that same persistence with one another and refuse to give up on colleagues who are slow to change.

All students can be motivated to learn. This is easy to believe when we see the eager faces of our kindergarten students, but after years of failure in school, or months of not understanding the language, our less-resilient, less-resourceful students often stop trying. They may be disruptive in class, have poor attendance, or simply not participate. We have all known students who dropped out of school years before they physically left it. Without thoroughly investigating a student's background, interests, and goals, a teacher might interpret his behavior with statements like these: "He's lazy." "All he cares about is getting on the soccer team."

A closer look via multiple methods of assessment will often reveal that the student suffers from a fear of failure stemming from repeated failure in the past. Armed with this knowledge, teachers can look for strengths and build from those. We are heartened by the research into the role that "grit" (hard work and persistence) plays in learning. The findings suggest that positive learning gains result when teachers make sure that their students understand that their effort and willingness to persist influence their achievement (see, for example, Blackwell, Trzesniewski, & Dweck, 2007; Duckworth, Peterson, Matthews, & Kelly, 2007). Persistence isn't just something we talk about, though—we need to embody it every day in our unwillingness as individuals and as systems to give up on a student.

All teachers are teachers of language. This principle is difficult to implement when the majority of teachers know little about language or language acquisition. These statements may sound familiar: "I don't have time to teach language—there's already too much to cover in the year." "It's not my job to teach grammar."

Clearly, institutions of higher education need to address this gap in their teacher education programs. A large part of the solution, however, lies in teachers' ability to tease out the language of mathematics or science, or whatever discipline they are teaching. Students need to be able to recognize the common language and text structures of each content area and the commonly used vocabulary in order to express their understanding of the content. The ongoing professional development within the professional learning community should focus on sound teaching practices. This is the knowledge base of teachers, and it needs continual refinement.

Values

As members of the school community, teachers and administrators have to examine their collective values and determine what they care about. As a starting point, we provide sample values and rationales for their adoption.

All students bring valuable skills and knowledge from their homes and cultures. In 1969, the President's Committee on Mental Retardation coined a new term: "the six-hour retarded child" (President's Committee on Mental Retardation & Bureau of Education for the Handicapped, 1969). The term referred to students whom the school had labeled "retarded" but who were competent in their communities and lives outside of their six hours in school. Society has changed dramatically since then, as have our values. Yet we can still find "six-hour disabled children." How do we view English learners? Do we value the funds of knowledge that serve them well in their lives outside of school? Do we view them as assets to our school, community, and nation? Or do we view them as a problem to solve? Answers to these questions require keen observation, honest reflection, open discussion, and some deep soul-searching.

In many classrooms it is not uncommon to observe English learners sitting quietly next to their peers, looking attentive but not actively participating. Well-meaning teachers who truly care about their students may make such comments as "They enter school with no language—not in English or their primary language" or "I don't want to embarrass them, so I don't call on them in class."

Well meant though they are, comments like these reveal a subtle culture of low expectations with little recognition of what it is that students *do* bring to the classroom. In the reauthorization of IDEA, the US Department of Education recognized that "implementation . . . has been impeded by low expectations" (IDEA, 20 U.S.C. § 1401(c)(4)). But what do high expectations look like in the classroom? It is not enough to say that we hold high expectations for all our students if this claim is not paired with action. In a classroom where EL students are held to high expectations, we would find evidence of these high expectations. We would see these students actively engaged, interacting with their peers, held accountable for meaningful and challenging work within collaborative tasks (beyond being the timekeeper), using resources in the room, and, importantly, using and producing language.

Diversity enriches our classrooms and our lives and has an important role in learning. What would we see in a classroom that places high value on diversity and recognizes that all students bring with them a worthy set of skills and knowledge, different though it may be from that of the mainstream culture? We would expect to see multicultural literature, translations of important words into the home languages of the students, collaborative work between students of different cultures, student choice in reading and projects, multiple manners of assessment, discussion about the similarities as well as the differences among cultures, and more. Just as, historically, immigrants have enriched our culture, English learners add to the richness of our classrooms and our society. Teachers need to know as much as they can about the cultures of their students. There is a wealth of information on the Internet, and the students themselves, of course, are excellent sources of information about their cultures, languages, and home countries. Clearly, teachers cannot be expected to know everything about every culture. Just as clearly, they should be open to learning about their students.

Practices

The instructional framework we have described in this book is based on the gradual release of responsibility model and includes teacher modeling, guided instruction, productive group work, and independent tasks. Within this framework, we have described nine key elements of effective instruction—whether language instruction or content instruction—for English learners:

1 *Clearly defined purpose*—Students understand the purpose of the lesson and how it relates to previous learning, their own lives, and future experiences.

2 *Models*—Students see clear demonstrations and examples of the process or skill they will learn and the product they will create.

3 *Interaction*—There are multiple opportunities for students to interact and talk with one another about the content in different ways.

4 *Guided instruction*—Time is built into the lesson for the teacher to work with small groups of students who have similar instructional needs. The teacher uses instructional scaffolds and differentiated instruction to guide students' understanding.

5 *Focus on language*—Lesson objectives include explicit instruction in language and vocabulary. Lessons require students to use all four domains of language—listening, speaking, reading, and writing—and offer scaffolds appropriate to the students' English proficiency levels.

6 *A culturally responsive curriculum*—Every student brings a rich bank of experiences that are influenced by culture, language, traditions, and social roles. When children's experiences closely match the teacher's, making the curriculum responsive for them is easier. However, our classrooms are filled with students with a variety of backgrounds and experiences. It is incumbent upon every teacher to become educated about the community's cultures in order to become more effective in the classroom.

7 *Meaningful and challenging tasks*—Students are engaged in work that has personal relevance or real-world application whenever possible. Teachers hold high expectations for learning and require students to use critical thinking skills. Challenging tasks that address grade-level standards are supported with differentiated resources, processes, or products that match students' instructional needs, personal interests and learning styles.

8 *Metacognition*—Students reflect on their learning, are aware of how they learn, and know where they stand in their progress toward their goals.

9 *Student choice*—Students choose from a menu of resources, projects, and assessments. Assignments and resources reflect the cultural diversity of the classroom.

Effective instruction for English learners requires far more than instituting a daily round of interactive activities. Of course, teachers need a repertoire of instructional routines to provide multiple opportunities for students to interact with one another and with the content. We also know that this repertoire can become little more than a bag of tricks that keep students entertained unless it is part of a plan, a plan that is based on a deep understanding of the concepts of teaching EL students.

It can be difficult to hold open and honest discussions about personal values, beliefs, and practices. Few educators would be willing to admit that they don't believe that all students can learn, for instance, even if they thought this premise to be more platitude than truth. Various experts have defined the problem; now it's time to focus on the solutions. And that's what this book is about—solutions for teaching English learners so that they reach the high expectations we have for them.

References

Abedi, J. (2004). The No Child Left Behind Act and English language learners: Assessment and accountability issues. *Educational Researcher, 33*(1), 4–14.

Algozzine, R., & Ysseldyke, J. (2006). *The fundamentals of special education: A practical guide for every teacher.* Thousand Oaks, CA: Corwin Press.

Ardoin, S. P., Witt, J. C., Connell, J. E., & Koenig, J. L. (2005). Application of a three-tiered response to intervention model for instructional planning, decision making, and the identification of children in need of services. *Journal of Psychoeducational Assessment, 23,* 362–380.

Asher, J. J. (1966). The total physical response: A review. *Modern Language Journal, 50*(2), 79–84.

Au, K. (2009). Isn't culturally responsive teaching just good teaching? *Social Education, 73*(4), 179–183.

August, D., & Shanahan, T. (Eds.). (2006). *Developing literacy in second-language learners: Report of the National Literacy Panel on Language-Minority Children and Youth.* Mahwah, NJ: Erlbaum.

Barrie, J. M. (2003). *Peter Pan* (Centennial ed.). New York: Henry Holt.

Barton, R., & Stepanek, J. (2009). Three tiers to success. *Principal Leadership, 9*(8), 16–20.

Bateman, B., & Herr, C. (2006). *Writing measurable IEP goals and objectives.* Verona, WI: Attainment.

Beavers, J. (1999). *Developmental reading assessment.* Parsippany, NJ: Celebration.

Berger, B. (2001). A systematic approach to grammar instruction. *Voices from the Middle, 8*(3), 43–49.

Blackwell, L., Trzesniewski, K., & Dweck, C. S. (2007). Implicit theories of intelligence predict achievement across an adolescent transition: A longitudinal study and an intervention. *Child Development, 78,* 246–263.

Brice, R. G., & Brice, A. E. (2009). Investigation of phonemic awareness and phonic skills in Spanish-English bilingual and English-speaking kindergarten students. *Communication Disorders Quarterly, 30*(4), 208–225.

Britton, J. (1983). Writing and the story of the world. In B. Kroll & E. Wells (Eds.), *Explorations in the development of writing theory, research, and practice* (pp. 3–30). New York: Wiley.

Brown, J. E., & Doolittle, J. (2008). *A cultural, linguistic, and ecological framework for response to intervention with English language learners.* Tempe, AZ: National Center for Culturally Responsive Educational Systems.

Buffum, A., Mattos, M., & Weber, C. (2009). *Pyramid response to intervention: RTI, professional learning communities, and how to respond when kids don't learn.* Bloomington, IN: Solution Tree Press.

Butler, Y. G., & Hakuta, K. (2009). The relationship between academic oral proficiency and reading performance: A comparative study between English learners and English-only students. *Reading Psychology, 30*(5), 412–444.

California Department of Education. (2009). *Determining specific learning disability eligibility using response to instruction and intervention (RTI2).* Sacramento, CA: Author.

Canale, M. (1983). Communicative competence to communicative language pedagogy. In J. Richards & R. Schmidt (Eds.), *Language and communication* (pp. 2–27). New York: Longman.

Canale, M., & Swain, M. (1980). Theoretical bases of communicative approaches to second language teaching and testing. *Applied Linguistics, 1*(1), 1–47.

Carle, E. (2008). *The very hungry caterpillar.* New York: Philomel.

Case, R. E., & Taylor, S. S. (2005). Language difference or learning disability? Answers from a linguistic perspective. *Clearing House, 78,* 127–130.

Castagnera, E., Fisher, D., Rodifer, K., Sax, C., & Frey, N. (2003). *Deciding what to teach and how to teach it: Connecting students through curriculum and instruction* (2nd ed.). Colorado Springs, CO: PEAK.

Chall, J. S., & Jacobs, V. A. (2003). Poor children's fourth grade slump. *American Educator, 27*(1), 14–15, 44.

Chall, J. S., Jacobs, V. A., & Baldwin, L. E. (1990). *The reading crisis: Why poor children fall behind.* Cambridge, MA: Harvard University Press.

Chamot, A. (2005). The cognitive academic language learning approach (CALLA): An update. In P. Richard-Amato & M. Snow (Eds.), *Academic success for English language learners* (pp. 87–101). White Plains, NY: Longman.

Christelow, E. (1998). *Five little monkeys jumping on a bed.* Boston: Houghton Mifflin Harcourt Children's Books.

Clay, M. M. (2006). *An observation survey of early literacy achievement* (Rev. 2nd ed.). Portsmouth, NH: Heinemann.

Collier, V. (1987). Age and rate of acquisition of second language for academic purposes. *TESOL Quarterly, 21*(4), 617–641.

Collier, V. P., & Thomas, W. P. (2004). The astounding effectiveness of dual language education for all. *NABE Journal of Research and Practice, 2*(1), 1–19.

Cosentino de Cohen, C., Deterding, N., & Clewell, B. C. (2005). *Who's left behind? Immigrant children in high- and low-LEP schools.* Washington, DC: Urban Institute.

Cummins, J. (1979). Cognitive/academic language proficiency, linguistic interdependence, the optimum age question and some other matters. *Working Papers on Bilingualism, 19,* 121–129.

Davey, B. (1987). Think aloud: Modeling cognitive processes for reading comprehension. *Journal of Reading, 27,* 44–47.

Deno, S. L. (1985). Curriculum-based measurement: The emerging alternative. *Exceptional Children, 52*(3), 219–232.

Diercks-Gransee, B., Weissenburger, J. W., Johnson, C. L., & Christensen, P. (2009). Curriculum-based measures of writing for high school students. *Remedial and Special Education, 30*(6), 360–371.

Dockrell, J., Lindsay, G., & Connelly, V. (2009). The impact of specific language impairment on adolescents' written text. *Exceptional Children, 75*(4), 427–446.

Dong, Y. R. (2004/2005). Getting at the content. *Educational Leadership, 62*(4), 14–19.

Duckworth, A. L., Peterson, C., Matthews, M. D., & Kelly, D. R. (2007). Grit: Perseverance and passion for long-term goals. *Journal of Personality and Social Psychology, 9*, 1087–1101.

DuFour, R., DuFour, R., Eaker, R., & Karhanek, G. (2004). *Whatever it takes: How professional learning communities respond when kids don't learn.* Bloomington, IN: Solution Tree Press.

Dutro, S. (2007, January). *A focused approach to instruction for English learners.* Paper presented at the Riverside County Office of Education English Learner Symposium, Riverside, CA. Accessed at www.rcoe.k12.ca.us/newsroom/archive/ELL/Dutro_RCOE%20 to%20post.pdf on June 18, 2010.

Dutro, S., & Moran, C. (2003). *Rethinking English language instruction: An architectural approach.* Newark, DE: International Reading Association.

Echevarria, J., & Hasbrouck, J. (2009). *Response to intervention and English learners.* Accessed at www.cal.org/create/resources/pubs/CREATEBrief_ResponsetoIntervention.pdf on June 18, 2010.

Elbaum, B., Vaughn, S., Hughes, M. T., & Moody, S. (2000). How effective are one-to-one tutoring programs in reading for elementary students at risk for reading failure? A meta-analysis of the intervention research. *Journal of Educational Psychology, 92*, 605–619.

Ellis, R. (2006). Current issues in the teaching of grammar: An SLA perspective. *TESOL Quarterly, 40*(1), 83–108.

Equal Educational Opportunities Act, 20 U.S.C. § 1703 (1974).

Fawson, P. C., Ludlow, B. C., & Reutzel, R. D. (2006). Examining the reliability of running records: Attaining generalizable results. *Journal of Educational Research, 100*(2), 113–126.

Feinberg, R. C. (2000). Newcomer schools: Salvation or segregated oblivion for immigrant students? *Theory Into Practice, 39*(4), 220–227.

Fisher, D., & Frey, N. (Eds.). (2004). *Inclusive urban schools.* Baltimore, MD: Paul H. Brookes.

Fisher, D., & Frey, N. (2007). *Checking for understanding: Formative assessments for your classroom.* Alexandria, VA: Association for Supervision and Curriculum Development.

Fisher, D., & Frey, N. (2008). *Better learning through structured teaching: A framework for the gradual release of responsibility.* Alexandria, VA: Association for Supervision and Curriculum Development.

Fisher, D., & Frey, N. (2009a). *Background knowledge: The missing piece of the comprehension puzzle.* Portsmouth, NH: Heinemann.

Fisher, D., & Frey, N. (2009b). Feed up, back, forward. *Educational Leadership, 67*(3), 20–25.

Fisher, D., & Frey, N. (2010). *Guided instruction: Questions, prompts, cues, and explanations.* Alexandria, VA: Association for Supervision and Curriculum Development.

Fisher, D., Frey, N., & Lapp, D. (2009). *In a reading state of mind: Brain research, teacher modeling, and comprehension instruction.* Newark, DE: International Reading Association.

Fisher, D., Frey, N., & Rothenberg, C. (2008). *Content area conversations: How to plan discussion-based lessons for diverse language learners.* Alexandria, VA: Association for Supervision and Curriculum Development.

Frayer, D. A., Frederick, W. C., & Klausmeier, H. J. (1969). *A schema for testing the level of concept mastery* (Working Paper No. 16). Madison, WI: Wisconsin Research and Development Center for Cognitive Learning.

Frey, N. (2006). The role of 1:1 individual instruction in reading. *Theory Into Practice, 45*(3), 207–214.

Frey, N. (2010). Home is not where you live, but where they understand you. In K. Dunsmore & D. Fisher (Eds.), *Bringing literacy home* (pp. 42–52). Newark, DE: International Reading Association.

Frey, N., Fisher, D., & Everlove, S. (2009). *Productive group work: How to engage students, build teamwork, and promote understanding.* Alexandria, VA: Association for Supervision and Curriculum Development.

Frey, N., Lapp, D., & Fisher, D. (2009). The academic booster shot: In-school tutoring to prevent grade-level retention. In J. Richards & C. Lassonde (Eds.), *Literacy tutoring that works: A look at successful in-school, after-school, and summer programs* (pp. 32–45). Newark, DE: International Reading Association.

Fuchs, D., & Fuchs, L. S. (2009). Responsiveness to intervention: Multilevel assessment and instruction as early intervention and disability identification. *Reading Teacher, 63,* 250–252.

Fuchs, L. S., & Fuchs, D. (1992). Identifying a measure for monitoring student reading progress. *School Psychology Review, 21,* 45–58.

Fuchs, L. S., & Fuchs, D. (2006). Implementing responsiveness-to-intervention to identify learning disabilities. *Perspectives on Dyslexia, 32*(1), 39–43.

Gaiman, N. (2002). *Coraline.* New York: HarperTrophy.

Gansle, K. A., VanDerHayden, A. M., Noell, G. H., Resetar, J. L., & Williams, K. L. (2006). The technical adequacy of curriculum-based and ratings-based measures of written expression for elementary students. *School Psychology Review, 35*(4), 435–450.

Garcia, G. (1991). Factors influencing the English reading test performance of Spanish-speaking Hispanic children. *Reading Research Quarterly, 26,* 371–392.

Gascoigne, C. (2002). *The debate on grammar in second language acquisition: Past, present, and future.* Lewiston, NJ: Edwin Mellen Press.

Gay, G. (2000). *Culturally responsive teaching: Theory, research, and practice.* New York: Teachers College Press.

Gladwell, M. (2005). *Blink: The power of thinking without thinking.* New York: Little, Brown and Company.

Goldenberg, C. (2008). Teaching English language learners: What the research does—and does not—say. *American Educator, 32*(2), 8–23, 42–44.

Graff, G., & Birkenstein, C. (2006). *They say/I say: The moves that matter in academic writing.* New York: W. W. Norton.

Graves, M. F., & Fitzgerald, J. (2003). Scaffolding reading experiences for multilingual classrooms. In G. G. Garcia (Ed.), *English learners: Reaching the highest level of English literacy* (pp. 96–124). Newark, DE: International Reading Association.

Greenfield, P. M. (1999). Historical change and cognitive change: A two-decade follow-up study in Zincantan, a Maya community in Chiapas, Mexico. *Mind, Culture, and Activity, 6,* 92–98.

Gutierrez-Clellen, V. F., & Peña, E. (2001). Dynamic assessment of diverse children: A tutorial. *Language, Speech, and Hearing Services in Schools, 32,* 212–224.

Hammill, D. D., & Newcomer, P. L. (2005). *Test of oral language development: Primary* (4th ed.). Boston: Pearson.

Harper, C., & De Jong, E. (2004). Misconceptions about teaching English-language learners. *Journal of Adolescent & Adult Literacy, 48*(2), 152–162.

Harry, B., & Klingner, J. K. (2005). *Why are so many minority students in special education? Understanding race and disability in schools.* New York: Teachers College Press.

Hasbrouck, J. (2006). Putting fluency in perspective. *Balanced Reading Instruction, 13,* 9–22.

Hasbrouck, J., & Tindal, G. (2006, April). Oral reading fluency norms: A valuable assessment tool for reading teachers. *Reading Teacher, 59,* 636–644.

Hill, J. D., & Flynn, K. M. (2006). *Classroom instruction that works with English language learners.* Alexandria, VA: Association for Supervision and Curriculum Development.

Illinois ASPIRE. (2009, December). *Reading and response to intervention: Putting it all together.* Accessed at www.illinoisaspire.org/welcome/files/Reading_RtI_Guide .pdf on June 10, 2010.

Individuals with Disabilities Education Act, 20 U.S.C. §§ 1400 *et.seq.* (2009). Accessed at www.ed.gov/about/offices/list/osers/osep/index.html on July 20, 2009.

International Reading Association. (2010). *Response to intervention: Guiding principles for educators.* Accessed at www.reading.org/Libraries/Resources/RTI_brochure_web.sflb.ashx on June 3, 2010.

Janney, R., & Snell, M. (2004). *Modifying schoolwork* (2nd ed.). Baltimore, MD: Brookes.

Johnson, E., Mellard, D. F., Fuchs, D., & McKnight, M. A. (2006). *Responsiveness to intervention (RTI): How to do it.* Lawrence, KS: National Research Center on Learning Disabilities. Accessed at www.nrcld.org/rti_manual/index.html on June 10, 2010.

Johnston, P. (2010). An instructional frame for RTI. *Reading Teacher, 63*(7), 602–604.

Jones, S. J. (2007). Culturally responsive instruction. *Leadership, 37*(2), 14–17, 36.

Jorgensen, C., McSheehan, M., & Sonnenmeier, R. (2009). *The beyond access model: Promoting membership, participation, and learning for students with disabilities in the general education classroom.* Baltimore, MD: Brookes.

Kern, R. (2000). *Literacy and language teaching.* New York: Oxford University Press.

Khan, C., & Mellard, D. (2008). *RTI in the language of a classroom teacher: Improving student success through collaboration.* Lawrence, KS: National Center on Response to Intervention.

Klingner, J. K., & Edwards, P. A. (2006). Cultural considerations with response to intervention models. *Reading Research Quarterly, 41*(1), 108–117.

Kolb, B., & Whishaw, I. Q. (2003). *Fundamentals of human neuropsychology* (5th ed.). New York: Worth.

Kuder, S. J. (2007). Teaching students with language and communication disabilities (3rd ed.). Boston: Allyn & Bacon.

Lambeth, E. (2008). Desert jaws! *Ranger Rick, 42*(11), 8.

Lapp, D., Fisher, D. M., Flood, J., & Moore, K. (2002). "I don't want to teach it wrong": An investigation of the role families believe they should play in the early literacy development of their children. In D. Schallert, C. Fairbanks, J. Worthy, B. Maloch, & J. Hoffman (Eds.), *51st Yearbook of the National Reading Conference* (pp. 275–287). Oak Creek, WI: National Reading Conference.

Lapp, D., Fisher, D., & Jacobson, J. (2008). Useful instructional routines for adolescent English language learners' vocabulary development. *California Reader, 42*(1), 10–22.

Larson, K. (2006). *Hattie big sky.* New York: Delacorte.

Larson, M. (1996). Watch your language: Teaching standard usage to resistant and reluctant learners. *English Journal, 85*(7), 91–95.

Lee, O., Mahotiere, M., Salinas, A., Penfield, R. D., & Maerten-Rivera, J. (2009). Science writing achievement among English language learners: Results of three-year intervention in urban elementary schools. *Bilingual Research Journal, 32*(2), 153–167.

Leslie, L., & Caldwell, J. S. (2005). *Qualitative reading inventory* (4th ed.). Boston: Allyn & Bacon.

MacGinitie, W. H., MacGinitie, R. K., Maria, K., Dreyer, L. G., & Hughes, K. E. (2000). *Gates-MacGinitie reading tests* (4th ed.). Itasca, IL: Riverside.

Manyak, P., & Bauer, E. (2008). Explicit code and comprehension instruction for English learners. *Reading Teacher, 61*(5), 432–434.

Marzano, R. J. (2004). *Building background knowledge for academic achievement: Research on what works in schools.* Alexandria, VA: Association for Supervision and Curriculum Development.

McGovern, A. (1991). *If you sailed on the Mayflower in 1620.* New York: Scholastic.

McMaster, K. L., Wayman, M. M., & Cao, M. (2006). Monitoring the reading progress of secondary-level English learners: Technical features of oral reading and maze tasks. *Assessment for Effective Intervention, 31,* 17–31.

Minow, M. L. (2001). *Funding mechanisms in special education.* Accessed at www.cast.org /publications/ncac/ncac_funding.html on June 18, 2010.

Moss, C. M., & Brookhart, S. M. (2009). *Advancing formative assessment in every classroom: A guide for instructional leaders.* Alexandria, VA: Association for Supervision and Curriculum Development.

National Association of State Directors of Special Education. (2005). *Response to intervention: Policy considerations and implementation.* Alexandria, VA: Author.

National Center for Education Statistics. (2010). *The nation's report card: Reading 2009.* Washington, DC: Author. Accessed at http://nces.ed.gov/pubsearch/pubsinfo.asp?pubid= 2010458 on June 29, 2010.

Nippold, M. (2009). School-age children talk about chess: Does knowledge drive syntactic complexity? *Journal of Speech, Language, and Hearing Research, 52*(4), 856–871.

O'Day, J. (2009). Good instruction is good for everyone—or is it? English language learners in a balanced literacy approach. *Journal of Education for Students Placed at Risk, 14,* 97–119.

Office of English Language Acquisition, Language Enhancement, and Academic Achievement for Limited English Proficient Students. (2008). *Biennial report to Congress on the implementation of the Title III State Formula Grant Program: School years 2004–06.* Washington, DC: U.S. Department of Education.

Orosco, M., & Klingner, J. (2010). One school's implementation of RTI with English language learners: "Referring into RTI." *Journal of Learning Disabilities, 43*(3), 269–288.

Parrish, T. B. (2001). Who's paying the rising cost of special education? *Journal of Special Education Leadership, 14*(1), 4–12.

Pearson, P. D., & Gallagher, G. (1983). The gradual release of responsibility model of instruction. *Contemporary Educational Psychology, 8,* 112–123.

Peña, D. C. (2000). Parent involvement: Influencing factors and implications. *Journal of Educational Research, 94,* 42–54.

Peña, E. D., Gillam, R. B., Malek, M., Ruiz-Felter, R., Resendiz, M., Fiestas, C., & Sabel, T. (2006). Dynamic assessment of school-age children's narrative ability: An experimental investigation of classification accuracy. *Journal of Speech, Language, and Hearing Research, 49*(5), 1037–1057.

Peregoy, S. F., & Boyle, O. F. (1997). *Reading, writing, & learning in ESL.* New York: Longman.

Pianta, R. C., Belsky, J., Houts, R., & Morrison, F. (2007). Opportunities to learn in America's elementary classrooms. *Science, 315,* 1795–1796.

Piper, T. (2006). *Language and learning: Home and school years* (4th ed.). Columbus: Prentice Hall.

Prelock, P. A. (2000). Multiple perspectives for determining the roles of speech-language pathologists in inclusionary classrooms. *Language, Speech, and Hearing Services in Schools, 31*(3), 213–218.

President's Committee on Mental Retardation & Bureau of Education for the Handicapped. (1969). *Conference on the learning problems of inner city children.* Washington, DC: U.S. Office of Education.

Rainforth, B., & York-Barr, J. (1997). *Collaborative teams for students with severe disabilities: Integrating therapy and educational services* (2nd ed.). Baltimore, MD: Brookes.

Raphael, L. M., Pressley, M., & Mohan, L. (2008). Engaging instruction in middle school classrooms: An observational study of nine teachers. *Elementary School Journal, 109*(1), 61–81.

Rapides Parish Schools. (2010). *Progress monitoring checklist for English language learners (ELL).* Accessed at http://www.rapides.k12.la.us/esl/ESL_checklist.pdf on June 8, 2010.

Reiser, B. J. (2004). Scaffolding complex learning: The mechanisms of structuring and problematizing student work. *Journal of the Learning Sciences, 13*(3), 273–304.

Saunders, W. M., Foorman, B. R., & Carlson, C. D. (2006). Do we need a separate block of time for oral English language development in programs for English learners? *Elementary School Journal, 107*(2), 181–198.

Scarcella, R. (2003). *Accelerating academic English: A focus on the English learner.* Irvine, CA: University of California, Irvine.

Scherer, M. (2003). *Connecting to learn: Educational and assistive technology for people with disabilities.* Washington, DC: American Psychological Association.

Shinn, M. R., & Shinn, M. M. (2002). *AIMSweb training notebook: Administration and scoring of reading maze for use in general outcome measures.* Eden Prairie, MN: EDformation.

Short, D. J., & Fitzsimmons, S. (2007). *Double the work: Challenges and solutions to acquiring language and academic literacy for adolescent English language learners—A report to Carnegie Corporation of New York.* Washington, DC: Alliance for Excellent Education.

Slavin, R. E., & Calderon, M. (Eds.). (2001). *Effective programs for Latino students.* Mahwah, NJ: Erlbaum.

Smith, B. (1997). Virtual realia. *The Internet TESL Journal, 3*(7). Accessed at http://iteslj.org/Articles/Smith-Realia.html on June 18, 2010.

Stinnett, N., & DeFrain, J. (1985). *Secrets of strong families.* Boston: Little, Brown.

Swain, M. (1995). Three functions of output in second language learning. In G. Cook & B. Seidlhofer (Eds.), *Principles and practice in the study of language* (pp. 125–144). Oxford: Oxford University Press.

Teachers of English to Speakers of Other Languages (TESOL). (2006). *PreK–12 English language proficiency standards.* Alexandria, VA: TESOL. Available from http://iweb.tesol.org/Purchase/ProductDetail.aspx?Product_code=318.

Tharp, R. G. (1997). *From at-risk to excellence: Research, theory and principles for practice* (Research Report No. 1). Washington, DC: Center for Applied Linguistics, Center for Research on Education, Diversity and Excellence.

Thomas, W. P., & Collier, V. P. (2002). *A national study of school effectiveness for language minority students' long-term academic achievement.* Santa Cruz, CA: Center for Research on Education, Diversity and Excellence.

Tilly, W. D., III. (2002). The evolution of school psychology to science-based practices: Problem solving and the three-tiered model. In A. Thomas & J. Grimes (Eds.), *Best practices in school psychology V* (pp. 17–36). Bethesda, MD: National Association of School Psychologists.

US Department of Education (2006, August). *Regulations for IDEA 2004.* Accessed at www.wrightslaw.com/idea/law/idea.regs.subpartd.pdf on June 28, 2010.

US Department of Education, Office for Civil Rights. (2007). *Students with disabilities preparing for postsecondary education: Know your rights and responsibilities.* Washington, DC: Author.

Vaughn, S., & Linan-Thompson, S. (2003). Group size and time allotted to intervention: Effects for students with reading difficulties. In B. Foorman (Ed.), *Preventing and remediating reading difficulties: Bringing science to scale* (pp. 299–324). Baltimore: York Press.

Vaughn, S., & Ortiz, A. (n.d.). *Response to intervention in reading for English language learners.* Washington, DC: RTI Action Network. Accessed at www.rtinetwork .org/Learn/Diversity/ar/EnglishLanguage on June 10, 2010.

Videen, J., Deno, S., & Marston, D. (1982). *Correct word sequences: A valid indicator of proficiency in written expression* (Research Report No. 84). Minneapolis: University of Minnesota, Institute for Research on Learning Disabilities.

Wallace, C. (2007). Vocabulary: The key to teaching English language learners to read. *Reading Improvement, 44*(4), 189–193.

Watts-Taffe, S., & Truscott, D. M. (2000). Using what we know about language and literacy development for ESL students in the mainstream classroom. *Language Arts, 77,* 258–265.

Webb, S. A. (2009). The effects of pre-learning vocabulary on reading comprehension and writing. *Canadian Modern Language Review, 65,* 441–470.

What Works Clearinghouse. (2009). Best practice for RTI: Small group instruction for students making minimal progress (Tier 3). Accessed at www.readingrockets.org/article /30676 on June 10, 2010.

Wiggins, G., & McTighe, J. (2005). *Understanding by design* (2nd ed.). Alexandria, VA: Association for Supervision and Curriculum Development.

Wiley, H. I., & Deno, S. L. (2005). Oral reading and maze measures as predictors of success for English learners on a state standards assessment. *Remedial and Special Education, 26,* 207–214.

Winsor, P. (2007). Language experience in Belize: Exploring language experience for English language learners. *Journal of Reading Education, 33*(1), 29–36.

Wisconsin Center for Education Research. (2007). *WIDA: Mission & history.* Madison, WI: Author. Accessed at www.wida.us/aboutus/mission.aspx on June 4, 2010.

Wolf, M. A. (2007). *Proust and the squid: The story and science of the reading brain.* New York: HarperCollins.

Wolf, M. A., & Denckla, M. B. (2005). *Rapid automatized naming and rapid alternating stimuli test.* Austin, TX: PRO-ED.

World-Class Instructional Design and Assessment. (2007). *English language proficiency standards for English language learners in prekindergarten through grade 12.* Originally published 2004. Accessed at www.wida.us/standards/elp.aspx on June 18, 2010.

Young, K. M., & Leinhardt G. (1998). Writing from primary documents: A way of knowing in history. *Written Communication, 15,* 25–68.

Index

Literacy 2.0
Nancy Frey, Douglas Fisher, and Alex Gonzalez
Students in the 21st century must incorporate traditional
literacy skills into a mastery of technology for communicating
and collaborating in new ways. This book offers specific
teaching strategies for developing students' skills related to
acquiring, producing, and sharing information.
BKF373

40 Reading Intervention Strategies for K–6 Students
Elaine K. McEwan-Adkins
This well-rounded collection of reading intervention
strategies, teacher-friendly lesson plans, and adaptable
miniroutines will support and inform your RTI efforts. Many
of the strategies motivate all students as well as scaffold
struggling readers. Increase effectiveness by using the
interventions across grade-level teams or schoolwide.
BKF270

Making Math Accessible to English Language Learners
r4 Educated Solutions
Help English language learners build academic vocabulary
and proficiency in meaningful mathematics while keeping
the entire class engaged. A great tool for strengthening
classroom instruction, this manual offers research-based
strategies that address the affective, linguistic, and cognitive
needs of ELLs.
K–2 **BKF284**, 3–5 **BKF285**, 6–8 **BKF286**, 9–12 **BKF287**

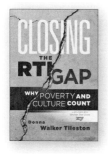

Closing the RTI Gap
Donna Walker Tileston
Get a clear understanding of poverty and culture, and learn
how RTI can close achievement gaps related to these issues.
Learn how you can achieve successful implementation
in your school. Examine common pitfalls to avoid in the
process.
BKF330

Solution Tree | Press   *a division of*
Solution Tree

Visit solution-tree.com or call 800.733.6786 to order.